In *Time Management Essentials,* Anna Dearmon Kornick does a magnificent job of cutting through all of the time management advice out there to find what actually works. Filled to the brim with practical, tactical advice, this is the book to pick up if you want to get better at managing your time—and find more energy and focus in the process. This book is well worth your time.

—**Chris Bailey,** bestselling author of *The Productivity Project, How to Calm Your Mind,* and *Hyperfocus*

Time Management Essentials is the modern time management playbook for spending time on what matters most. Anna distills values-based time management strategies into a comprehensive, easy to follow, and fun-to-read guide. This is a must-read for busy professionals who want to take charge of their time without wasting time in the process.

—**Nir Eyal,** bestselling author of *Indistractable* and *Hooked*

Time management doesn't have to be hard! In this engaging and reassuring book, Anna shares practical strategies that can help you get more done and enjoy your life at the same time.

—**Laura Vanderkam,** bestselling author of *Tranquility by Tuesday* and *168 Hours*

What I love about this book, and about Anna herself, is that it skips past all the nonsense—cheap tricks, tips, hacks, "must-do" lists—and addresses the real substance of time management: what's our purpose and how to construct our lives to fulfill that purpose. If you've been searching for substance, I could not recommend this book highly enough.

—**Matt Martin**, cofounder and CEO of Clockwise

This book hit me at exactly the right moment. As someone who spends so much time thinking about time, it was surprising and invigorating to learn that I had been winging it on so many things that deserved more attention. Anna gave me exactly what I needed to take my time management to the next level. Not only that—she had the courage to put vision and values first. She thoroughly covers not only the "how," but also the "why" behind time management in a beautiful blend of life-improving advice and inspiration. If you care about making the most out of your time, you owe it to yourself to read this book.

—**Ben Miller**, founder and CEO of ChroniFI

I love this book! *Time Management Essentials* is not about squeezing more work into the same number of hours—it's a step-by-step guide that helps you stop spending your time on nonessential busywork and start filling those hours with what matters to you most.

—**Minda Zetlin**, author of *Career Self-Care* and *The Geek Gap*, and writer of the highly popular "The Laid-Back Leader" column at Inc.com

TIME MANAGEMENT ESSENTIALS

TIME MANAGEMENT ESSENTIALS

THE TOOLS YOU NEED TO MAXIMIZE YOUR ATTENTION, ENERGY, AND PRODUCTIVITY

ANNA DEARMON KORNICK

NEW YORK CHICAGO SAN FRANCISCO ATHENS LONDON
MADRID MEXICO CITY MILAN NEW DELHI
SINGAPORE SYDNEY TORONTO

1 2 3 4 5 6 7 8 9 LCR 28 27 26 25 24 23

ISBN 978-1-264-98877-8
MHID 1-264-98877-X

e-ISBN 978-1-264-98886-0
e-MHID 1-264-98886-9

Design by Mauna Eichner and Lee Fukui

Library of Congress Cataloging-in-Publication Data

Names: Kornick, Anna Dearmon, author.
Title: Time management essentials : the tools you need to maximize your attention, energy, and productivity / Anna Dearmon Kornick.
Description: New York : McGraw Hill, [2023] | Includes bibliographical references and index.
Identifiers: LCCN 2022057274 (print) | LCCN 2022057275 (ebook) | ISBN 9781264988778 (hardback) | ISBN 9781264988860 (ebook)
Subjects: LCSH: Time management.
Classification: LCC HD69.T54 K67 2023 (print) | LCC HD69.T54 (ebook) | DDC --1/650.1dc23/eng/20230210
LC record available at https://lccn.loc.gov/2022057274
LC ebook record available at https://lccn.loc.gov/2022057275

McGraw Hill is committed to making our products accessible to all learners. To learn more about the available support and accommodations we offer, please contact us at accessibility@mheducation.com. We also participate in the Access Text Network (www.accesstext.org), and ATN members may submit requests through ATN.

To Scott, Mil, and Bit. You are what matters most.

Contents

PART III
BEYOND THE ESSENTIALS

Acknowledgments

Every time I finish reading a book, it's never really over until I read the Acknowledgments. After spending 200+ pages with the author, I just feel like I owe it to those who supported him or her along the way to read the pages of thanks.

The *Oxford English Dictionary* defines *acknowledgment* as "acceptance of the truth or existence of something." Now that I'm writing my own acknowledgments, it hardly feels like the most appropriate word to describe the immense and utter gratitude I feel. There are so many people who deserve a full-on parade with giant balloons, multiple marching bands, and intricately hand-painted, double-decker floats. A sentence or two hardly seems like enough.

First, I could not have dreamed of a better editor than Cheryl Segura. A fellow productivity enthusiast, Cheryl's patience, encouragement, and organization kept us moving forward. I'm grateful to her for taking a chance on me as a first-time author, and it was a delight to get to know her through the process of bringing this "book baby" into the world. She definitely made this experience much less stressful and much more fun than I imagined it would be! So glad Instagram brought us together and that we found each other in the DMs.

Many thanks to the entire team at McGraw Hill, particularly Pattie Amoroso for shepherding the book through the production process and Scott Sewell for the helpful marketing advice. Denise's quirky and fun illustrations bringing the concepts in this book to life were the icing on the cake.

Without Mauna Eichner and Lee Fukui overseeing the design, copyediting, composition, proofreading, and so much more, this book would still be a folder full of Word documents on my desktop. Thank you for consistently following up with me to bring these words into actual book form.

This book also wouldn't be possible without a few bold moves, and for that inspiration and encouragement, I'm grateful to my first "writer friend," Shanna Hocking. Minda Zetlin also gave me some fantastic advice for setting the mood and staying focused throughout the process.

The stories peppered throughout this book wouldn't have been possible without the trust of my clients and friends (and clients who have become friends). Thank you to Andree, Corinn, Liz, Kimberly, and others for allowing me to share your stories. The *It's About Time* podcast is the first place many of these stories and concepts were originally shared, and I'm grateful for every listener and supporter of the show, especially Kevin Chemidlin whose TDE framework changed everything.

Thank you to the team at Clockwise, particularly Fran, for believing in me and for being a true example of a company that lives its Values. I'll always be cheering you on, confetti and all, as you continue to help the world make time for what matters.

Without coffee and friends, I would still be stuck somewhere around Chapter 2. Thank you to Rhiannon and Lauren for gifting me with writing fuel, and to the entire team at Abita Coffee Works at Copperstill for making the best s'more lattes that kept me going during those rainy Sunday writing sessions. Writing and running an online business can be notoriously lonely (especially on rainy Sundays), but I've got the best sounding board in the Go-Getters Mastermind: Lauren Felter, Catherine Guidry, Stephanie Judice, and Kimberly Tara. Thank you to Sarah Becker for always making me look good and feel good behind the camera, and for asking so many great questions like we've known each other for way longer than just a few years. I can't imagine navigating the past few years of moves, motherhood, and business without Logan Doerries and our three to four simultaneous conversations on multiple topics across several platforms. And as sure as Kilimanjaro rises like Olympus above the Serengeti, I'm grateful that I could count on the Perry Como Social Club for comic relief during my five-minute Pomodoro breaks.

Teamwork makes the dream work, and I definitely couldn't have simultaneously published the podcast, coached clients, launched the It's About Time Academy, and written a book without Ally Carolan, Elisa McManus, Madeleine Herskind, and Latasha Doyle with her spectacular Uncanny Content team. Nor could I have peace of mind month to month without regular conversations with Kristen Ricupero.

Thank you to Maria for sharing with me the book that sparked my interest in time management, giving me proof of what's possible. Of course, if you'd told me then that one day I'd be writing my own book about time management I'd have fallen on the floor laughing.

Thank you to my dad for kicking off my competitive streak by never letting me win at checkers, and for teaching me that sometimes a walk around the block is exactly what you need to shake off the cobwebs and feel refreshed so you can get back to it. So often we think of time management as a tool for making space for more work, but you remind me that time should also be spent painting, playing games, and just spending time with people you love.

I'm very fortunate to have grown up with a mother who didn't just tell me that I could do anything I set my mind to, she actually believed it, reminded me of it, and then drove me there in her Suburban. We usually stopped at Sonic on the way. Thank you for your prayers, for worrying about me, and for always attending every single competition, event, performance, halftime show, pageant, conference, recital, and livestock exhibition. Your full calendar was a reflection of your full heart—supportive, loving, and always there.

When I say that I believe that time management starts with heart, my heart belongs to Scott, Camilla, and Elizabeth. When I say that we should spend our time based on what matters most, what matters most to me is Scott, Camilla, and Elizabeth. While I want to live like life is a marathon and not a sprint, I also know that we aren't promised tomorrow. When it all comes down to deciding what matters most, it's always the time I spend with you.

Thank you to my girls for giving me so much *joy* and adding fuel to my fire for making a difference in the world. I hope that you grow up believing that you can do anything, too.

My favorite part of the Acknowledgments is when the writer thanks their spouse. Often the writer apologizes for being a hermit for months while in writing mode, and acknowledges that it was their partner who kept the family train on the tracks. I get it now.

Without Scott, I would be starving and exhausted. Plus, I wouldn't laugh as often. Thank you for everything you do for our family and to support and encourage me, especially when I feel like the sky is falling. Thank you for being understanding when I needed yet another Sunday at the coffee shop to work through a chapter, and for being such an amazing dad to the girls. You give Bandit Heeler a run for his money.

Introduction: The Truth About Time Management

Put away your planner. Close your calendar. Set your to-do list to the side. You might even want to take off your watch for this. I'm about to share the secret to mastering time management, and it's probably not what you think it is.

After talking with thousands of people from all walks of life about how they spend their time, I've encountered many beliefs about what it means to be good at time management. Some believe that time management is about finding a way to fit more into a 24-hour day or drawing a thick line through every item on a to-do list with a sigh of relief and a feeling of accomplishment. Others think that good time management looks like doing as much as humanly possible—as if they're racing to reach an invisible finish line that's constantly moving farther away. For some, time management means cobbling together a hodgepodge of productivity hacks, shaving off a minute here or a minute there from day-to-day tasks. Still others strive to optimize every aspect of their lives to somehow save time, doing push-ups while brewing their morning coffee or outsourcing everything from grocery shopping to laundry to dog walking and beyond.

None of those ideas about time management is necessarily wrong. Personally, I love a good productivity hack. Plus, I'm a big fan of outsourcing and get a thrill from crossing things off of my to-do list.

But the most common belief, and perhaps the biggest misconception, is that good time management starts in the pages of a planner or in the small squares of a calendar.

We're going to approach time management from a different angle. We're going to zoom out. We'll step back from the planner and the calendar apps, the task management systems, and productivity hacks. Our focus will not be on the day-to-day (at least, not in the beginning).

The truth about time management is that it actually begins with Purpose. *Your* Purpose. When we zoom out and approach time management with a big-picture perspective—considering what we want out of life, instead of the next day or the next week—so many things will become easier in your life. Making decisions becomes easier. Cultivating new habits becomes easier. Managing your energy becomes easier. Knowing what to say yes or no to becomes easier. When you get crystal clear on your Purpose, on what matters most to you, everything feels easier.

Before you put down the book and roll your eyes, I challenge you to stick with me. You see, I was in your place once. Overwhelmed. Burned out. Scatterbrained and frantic. Living from one day to the next without a clear plan or a Vision for the future. I was the "late friend." You know, the one who gets a fake start time for get-togethers. "Tell Anna we're heading to dinner at 5:30 p.m. so she shows up by 6 p.m."

It gets worse. As a crisis communications pro clocking hours at a boutique public relations firm in New Orleans, I was written up by my boss for being late to work no less than 17 times in a six-month period. I missed deadlines and appointments, and let people down over and over again. It's fair to say that my time management woes were chronic; I was in dire need of a turnaround.

In an effort to make that happen, I dove headfirst into every book, article, resource, scholarly journal, and podcast I could find in search of some magic bullet that would help me manage my time. Slowly, I began implementing what I'd learned, and slowly I began to see results. Life felt simpler, calmer even. I woke up each day knowing exactly what needed to be done and how I would accomplish it. My confidence grew, and soon others noticed and asked me for advice.

Along my meandering path to understanding time management, I discovered a simple, repeatable method for transforming one's relationship with time. The path begins with defining your Purpose, casting your Vision for the future, and articulating personal Values. Then, priorities and goals guide day-to-day actions and activities. Minutes are maximized by combating productivity pitfalls with time-tested strategies. Finally, being organized, energized, focused, and rested enables you to further optimize your time for maximum efficiency and effectiveness.

Time management did not come naturally to me, and it doesn't have to come naturally to you, either. If I can transform from being the perpetually late friend to mastering time management, you absolutely can. Plus, think about the time you're saving by skipping the years of trial and error that I endured. You get to cut to the chase with a clear path from Purpose to productivity. Lucky you!

WHAT YOU'LL GET FROM THIS BOOK

Imagine stepping into each week feeling calm and prepared because you know exactly what you need to accomplish in the week ahead. You know when you'll tackle each item on your to-do list. You feel focused when you're working, and present when not working. If it sounds like a dream, it's not. It's absolutely possible when you understand the essentials of time management.

If you're beginning to feel optimistic, but you're still a bit skeptical about whether *you* can truly make time management a real part of your everyday life, you're not alone. The idea of perfectly managing your time, meticulously organizing your calendar, and finding space in your day for absolutely everything seems impossible. And it should, because it is. Time management perfection isn't our goal. Instead, by learning the essentials of time management you'll be equipped to make time management work for you and your life. Here's how we'll make that happen together before you close the last page of this book.

HOW THIS BOOK IS ORGANIZED

As you make your way through *Time Management Essentials*, you'll find three distinct parts.

Part I, "The Essentials," shares the foundational pieces for sustainable, Purpose-driven time management. Understanding these fundamental principles and potential pitfalls will shift your perspective of time management from simply watching the clock and updating your calendar to planning with Purpose and living with intention.

Part II, "Essentials Applied," begins with a self-assessment. Here, you'll take inventory of your time management strengths and opportunities for improvement, and then use the practical applications and step-by-step exercises in Chapters 5–7 to bring the fundamentals of time management to life.

In Part III, "Beyond the Essentials," you'll be equipped with helpful tips and strategies to enhance your new time management skills. From getting better sleep and maintaining concentration to creating organized systems and tapping into your natural energy, good time management goes beyond the pages of your calendar.

Together, these sections are your guide to creating a personalized strategy for time management success at work and in your life.

Isn't it about time you took control of your time?

Let's dive in!

TIME MANAGEMENT ESSENTIALS

PART I
THE ESSENTIALS

The Power of Purpose

In the hustle and bustle of our day-to-day lives, rarely do we pause to consider our life's Purpose. We're much too busy running errands, jumping on Zoom meetings, or picking up groceries to ponder whether we're living according to our Purpose. Who has time for that?

However, good time management is impossible without clearly knowing what matters most to you. If we skip past Purpose and instead dive straight into all the time management hacks (creating an Ideal Week, setting goals, and doing all the things that seem like quick fixes), we might accidentally quick fix our way into living a life we don't love.

If you don't take the time to define what's most important to you—your Purpose (which as we will learn is made up of your Vision and Values), your days and your life will be spent living *someone else's Purpose.*

I learned this the hard way. The beginning pages of nearly every planner I've ever purchased are filled with exercises that walk you through your Vision and goals for the year ahead and ask you to consider how you want to spend your year and what you hope to accomplish. Without fail, I skipped over these pages every time and got to work filling in my appointments and to-dos. (How many of you are with me here?)

And then, I wondered why I felt constantly swept up in a sea of meaningless obligations and resentful of requests for my time!

Instead of living with Purpose, I was living in default mode.

What's default mode? That's the way you feel when you're just going through the motions. You go to work and come home, following the equivalent of a well-worn path through your life. In default mode, you do things because that's the way you've always done them and you're likely so caught up in making everyone *else* happy that along the way you've lost touch with what you actually wanted out of life.

So, what *do* you want out of life?

That question might seem too big to answer now, but by the end of this chapter you'll have a response that gets you excited to get out of bed each day.

YOUR PURPOSE = YOUR VISION + VALUES

To get started, it's important to understand that your Purpose revolves around two things: your Vision and your Values. Your Vision is what you want your life to look like in the future. Your Values represent your highest priorities and deeply held beliefs. Together, your Vision and your Values anchor every decision you make about how to spend your time.

Still not clear on what separates your Vision from your Values? Think of it this way: If your Vision is the mental picture of the future you hope to create for yourself, your Values are the guiding principles that help you chart your course to that future. Your Vision gives you a direction to move in, and your Values influence the choices you make along the path to that Vision.

In this chapter, we'll define your big Vision for the future and articulate your Values through exercises, examples, and more. Let's kick off our Purpose work by clarifying your Vision.

YOUR VISION

Whether you're baking a cake, building a house, or envisioning your ideal life, we have to *think* about things before we can create them. Cakes begin with recipes. Homes are built with blueprints. Both begin as ideas—as someone's Vision. The same goes for your ideal life. You can't live your dream life unless you first articulate what exactly your dream life actually is! Whether you want a successful career, thriving business, happy family, or strong relationship, you've got to imagine what that successful career, thriving business, happy family, or strong relationship actually looks like so you can pursue it.

When you make a conscious effort to picture what you want in your mind—although it may seem like you're not really doing anything—you're actually taking control of your life and your circumstances.

Your Vision Guides Your Decisions and Gives You Hope

When you have a clear Vision, it becomes easier to make choices about how to spend your time—whether to accept a certain job, make a big move, or go out on that date—because either the choice fits into your Vision or it doesn't.

Having a Vision isn't just about having clarity around big decisions. Your Vision drives the small ones, too. If your Vision includes being a homeowner, your daily decisions might include checking in with your budget to make sure you're on track to hit your down payment goal. If your Vision includes having a successful business, you're more likely to stick to your business plan instead of going rogue, overspending, or throwing your to-do list out the window and heading to the golf course.

When you have a crystal-clear picture of what you want the future to look like, it's easier to make decisions that get you closer to making that future a reality.

It also gives you hope. Hope boosts your happiness, makes you more productive, and improves your health and well-being. It can even help you live longer. Hope gives you something to be excited about. When you're excited, your happiness increases and your health improves. You feel like life's worth living because you're heading somewhere.

How Do You Capture a Vision?

Now that we know the importance of a Vision and that it's a mental picture of what we want our future to look like, how exactly do we capture that? It's not as if we can send mental snapshots to the one-hour photo lab like we did with our bright yellow Kodak disposable cameras back in the 1990s. Instead, our Vision must be captured in other ways.

Whether you articulate your Vision in a succinct Vision statement, write a letter to yourself from "future you," or get crafty and create a Vision board, capturing your Vision so that it has a home outside of your daydreams is a critical step. That being said, regardless of *how* you capture it, your Vision is a description of the future you hope to create for yourself.

It's also important to realize that your Vision is personal to you. It can be big-picture and long-term (encompassing all aspects of your personal life, work, relationships, and health) or more immediate and short-term (for something like your travel plans in the upcoming year). Your Vision can live in a bulleted list, divided up into different categories. Your Vision might be written out in paragraph form. It can be a scribbled stream of consciousness in the pages of your journal, or it can be neatly typed in a Google Doc.

If you've ever felt intimidated by the thought of creating a Vision for your life, I hope the exercises below help you tremendously and give you a sense of relief. There's no one right way to create a Vision, and in the following exercises, you can test-drive different methods for clarifying and capturing your Vision.

Exercise 1: The Story of You

What kind of life do *you* hope to look back on as you near the end of your days? What kind of stories do you want to tell? Will you have experiences and adventures that depict a life well-lived? Or, will you look back with regret over the things you *didn't* do, the missed opportunities, or the choices you made based on what everyone else wanted for you or from you.

Picture yourself, decades from now. Maybe you're in your 80s, sitting on your front porch in a rocking chair, enjoying a glass of lemonade. I like to imagine myself on our back patio at home, sipping sweet tea with a fluffy dog in my lap, watching the sunset with my husband, Scott. Maybe you'll picture yourself on a Jet Ski in Mexico or floating above Paris in a hot-air balloon. Regardless of where you are, get that picture in your mind right now.

Set the scene. What are you wearing? Are you listening to music? What time of day is it? What's the weather like? Put yourself as vividly into the future as you can.

Next, picture yourself chatting with someone in that setting. It could be your spouse, your children, a good friend, a neighbor, or someone else important to you. As you sit together, you reminisce and tell stories from the past, stories about the full life you've led.

Suddenly, a car drives up and a young woman steps out of the car and walks up to greet you. She's a biographer, and she's come to interview you to write a book about your life. Oh yes, you're a big deal. She sits down, opens her notebook, and places a small recording device on the table between you.

Now, take a moment to answer each of these questions:

- Why is this biographer writing about you?
- What are the big chapters in your life's story?
- What was your biggest achievement?
- What are you most proud of?
- What are you known for?
- What were some of the lowest points in your life?
- How did you get through them?
- What was your biggest life lesson?
- What was the pinnacle of your career?
- What did you create?
- How did you spend your time when you weren't working?

- Did you have hobbies, like cooking or pottery or improv?
- What legacy will you leave for friends and family?
- And finally, what's the name of your biography?

Once you've had an opportunity to answer these questions, take a moment to reflect on your answers. Is this the story you hope to tell when you're 80? Are you taking steps now in your day-to-day life to make this Vision a reality? Or, are you saving the good stuff and the big moves for "someday" when you finally have time, or when it's more convenient?

Author Bob Goff once tweeted, "The battle for our hearts are fought on the pages of our calendars." Getting crystal clear about the life you want to look back on with gratitude when you're 80 is a solid step toward winning that battle and living a life with no regrets.

Once you've completed this exercise and chosen the title of your biography, write your title on a sticky note and post it where you can see it. Whenever you see your biography title, you'll be reminded of the stories you want to tell and feel energized to make decisions and take the small daily actions that will move you one step closer to your Vision for the future.

Exercise 2: To You; From You

The email from my client read:

> It took me a while to sit down and write this letter because I wanted to give it the proper energy. But also, I was afraid to face the words that I'd be writing. Letting myself be vulnerable on a page means I also have to face what I really want out of life.

What do *you* really want out of life? There's no doubt that facing a question about life that's this big can be intimidating. However, as the years go by, we usually become wiser with experience. Think about past milestones in your life. Graduating from high school, graduating from college, having your first child, moving to a new home or state, starting your first job, or opening your business are all major turning points in people's lives. Traversing these milestones comes with mistakes, achievements, and lessons learned. What advice would you give a younger version of yourself approaching one of these milestones? What have you learned that you wish you had known back then?

In this exercise, you'll write a letter. This letter is to you in the present, from you in the future. No, we aren't stepping into a time machine to arrive at a point years from now in which you've achieved your goals and earned the wisdom that comes from living life. Instead, we're going to imagine life five years from now.

Picture you, five years in the future. You wake up each day feeling calm and prepared. You're loving life. You're fulfilled in your work, with your family, and with how you spend your time. Each day is filled with Purpose, and you close your eyes at night feeling satisfied and ready for tomorrow. You have solid routines in place, you're achieving your goals in health, wellness, relationships, personal development, community service, and beyond. You're feeling great. You're happier than ever.

You look back on the past five years and think about how far you've come, so you sit down to write a letter to "five years ago you."

In your letter, describe what life looks like *now*. Describe how you spend your days, and how amazing things have turned out. Share your wins, and what you're most proud of. Make sure you also note that life during these past five years wasn't always sunshine and rainbows. Tell "five years ago you" about the challenges and obstacles you encountered along the way. Tell yourself about the highs *and* the lows as you were making your way through the years. What did you learn? What sacrifices did you make? How did you get out of your comfort zone? What did you do differently? What do you regret? What did you add, and what did you let go of? What do you think you changed to get to this point?

End your letter by telling yourself what's next. Share what's on the horizon for the next five years and beyond. Go into detail about the plans you have for yourself, and how you'll get there. Encourage "five years ago you" and share the advice you wish someone would give you today. Then, sign your letter.

After you've written your letter, read and reread it. You may want to tuck your letter in a safe place so you can read it when you need encouragement and want to be reminded of the Vision you have for your life. This exercise has been so powerful for so many of my clients and I truly hope it's the same for you. In fact, one client who did this exercise in spring 2020 kept her Vision top of mind by writing "2025" on an index card and posting it on her bathroom mirror so she'd see it each morning and remember to believe in herself and her Vision for the future.

• • •

While I hope these two exercises start you on your path to clarifying your Vision, there are many more ways to capture how you hope to spend your time. You can condense your Vision for the future into a sentence or two, called a Vision statement. You can also create a Vision board, which is a compilation of images that represent the different activities and ideas within your big Vision.

Regardless of *how* you capture your Vision, what's important is that you spend time thinking through the future you hope to create for yourself. Then, keep your Vision visible. Just like the 2025 index card example, create a reminder of your Vision that you can see frequently. Post your Vision board near your desk. Create a desktop background featuring your Vision statement. When your Vision is top of mind, it can inspire your decisions throughout your daily life.

YOUR VALUES

In the smash hit Broadway production *Hamilton: An American Musical,* Lin Manuel Miranda's Alexander Hamilton asks antagonist Aaron Burr, "If you stand for nothing, Burr, what will you fall for?"

Your Values are what you stand for. They're your North Star and guiding principles as you move through life. If you haven't articulated your Values, you're at a disadvantage when it comes to making decisions of all shapes and sizes. Just like having a clear Vision in mind when making decisions is important, knowing your Values and measuring opportunities against those Values is critical, too—whether it's a job opportunity, potential client, meeting request, leadership role, or hot date. By deeply knowing and living by your Values, you can quickly determine if something is, or isn't, worth your precious time.

In August 2021, I was faced with a decision I never could have predicted. After leaving traditional employment, giving up my W-2 and employee badge in 2016, I spent five years building and growing my business as a time management coach. When an email from a guy named Fran with a company called Clockwise hit my inbox asking if I'd be interested in discussing a full-time role with the company, I was certain my spam filter was on the fritz. However, after weeks of conversations with Fran and others on the Clockwise team, returning to the world of full-time employment was a no-brainer.

Clockwise's Values are empathy, authenticity, focus, drive, curiosity, and enthusiasm. It was clear to me in my interactions with the Clockwise team that their Values were more than just nice words paired with cute graphics posted on their Careers page. Their Values permeated every aspect of the recruiting process, and every single person I spoke with seemed to radiate those Values.

Knowing my Values made what could have been an agonizing decision quite simple.

What Do Values Look Like?

So, how can you define your Values? In just five steps, we'll do exactly that. Before we get started, though, it's important to know that your Values don't have to be deep or profound, but they should be steadfast and consistent. Additionally, Values should only consist of five to seven words that represent what's most important to you. Having too many can dilute their power and diminish their meaning. We're articulating our Values, not making a list of nice words that sound good.

With that, let's get to work!

Step 1: Make a List of 100 Dreams

The first book I ever read about time and time management was *168 Hours* by Laura Vanderkam. In that book, Vanderkam shares a brainstorming exercise she learned from career coach Caroline Ceniza-Levine. Ceniza-Levine has her clients create a list of 100 dreams—a completely unedited list of anything one might want to do, have, or experience during their lifetime. Creating your own list of 100 dreams is a fun and effective way to further crystallize your Vision and begin our process of articulating your Values. Plus, it's fun to let yourself dream for a bit.

The instructions are simple. Jot down 100 things you'd like to experience, places you'd like to travel to, or goals you'd like to accomplish. This can even include relationships you'd like to cultivate or books you'd like to read. Feel free to include big dreams you've already accomplished because they count, too!

The benefit and challenge of compiling a list of 100 dreams is that you have to be specific. Just writing "Travel more" doesn't cut it, and it'll take you a really long time to get to 100 if you're being overly general. Let yourself totally go. Dream big for yourself!

As you get to work, here's a tip if you're feeling stuck: set a timer for 15 minutes and write down as many dreams as possible until the timer goes off. Then, leave your list out where you can easily add to it throughout the day or week. Then, just keep adding to it until you get to 100.

As you're compiling your list of 100 dreams, keep in mind that this list is about you, and only you. This is what *you* want, not what you think you should want or what others want for you. Give yourself the gift of being selfish with your list of 100 dreams. This is your space to dream, so give it your all.

Step 2: Identify Your Dream Themes

Once you've made your list of 100 dreams, it's time to reflect. Look over the dreams you've captured. Do you see any themes or patterns as you review your dreams? What do the items on your list have in common? Can you create categories for similar dreams? If so, which dreams can be grouped together?

Use this step to get messy with your list. Circle, star, highlight, underline, or rewrite your list—do whatever it takes to sort your dreams into groups. Once you've sorted your dreams into different categories, give each category a name. I call these groupings your Dream Themes, and they form the basis of your Values.

For example, maybe you have several travel-related or home improvement dreams. Or, you see lots of creative projects, books, paintings, or experiences on your dreams list. Perhaps there's a focus on dreams around relationships or career-building. All of these could be made into Dream Themes that will help you get closer to clarifying your Values.

Before we move to the next step, here's a gut check question: Does how you spend your time now reflect those dreams? This part is usually when people begin to realize what truly matters to them, and that the things they hope to experience in the future are hardly present in their day-to-day lives. This is a step toward changing that.

Step 3: Choose Your Words

Once you've identified your Dream Themes by batching your dreams into different categories, start brainstorming words or phrases that represent those themes. For example, if one of your Dream Themes centers around relationships, maybe "acceptance" or "teamwork" is a value for you.

Use the Values word list below as inspiration. Write down any words that feel right. Circle words or put a star next to some. Draw a line through words that definitely don't make your list.

abundance
acceptance
accomplishment
accuracy
achievement
acknowledgment
active
adaptability
adventure
affection
affluence
agility
ambition
appreciation
assertive
attractive
awareness
balance
beauty
best

belonging
bold
boundless
brave
bright
brilliant
calm
challenge
charity
charm
clarity
comfort
commitment
compassion
completion
composure
connection
control
cooperation
correct
courage
creativity
credibility
curiosity
daring
decisive
dependable
determined
devotion
diligence
diplomacy
discovery
diversity
drive
duty
education
effective
efficient
elegance
excitement
experience
expertise
expression
fairness
faith
fame
family
fearless
fitness
focus
freedom
fun
generosity
grace
gratitude
growth
happiness
harmony
health
honesty
humility
humor
imagination
inclusivity
independence
inspiration
integrity
intelligence
intuition
joy
justice
kindness
knowledge
leadership
learning
liberty
logic
love
loyalty
mindfulness
motivation
obedience
open-mindedness
optimism
organization
originality
passion
peace
philanthropy
playfulness
popularity
power
pragmatism
precision
professionalism
reason
recognition
reliable
resilience
resourcefulness
respect
self-control
selflessness
self-reliance
service
significance
simplicity
spirituality
spontaneity
strength
success
support
teamwork
tradition
truth
unique
victory
vision
warmth
wisdom

Step 4: Narrow the List Down

At this point, you've probably assembled a lengthy list of words and phrases that represent your Dream Themes and what matters most to you. Since your Values should typically be a list of five to seven words, it's time to narrow down your list. Slowly review your list, taking a moment to consider every word. Ask yourself these questions about each word:

- What does this word mean to me?
- What does this represent in my life right now?
- What do I hope this word will represent in the future?
- How would I feel if this word was not included in my Values?

Remember, your Values are not a collection of nice words. They represent the ideas and beliefs that make you, *you*. Once you've reviewed each meaningful word, narrow down your list to 10 or fewer. Then, rank your remaining words in order of importance.

Step 5: Reflect and Refine

Now that you've narrowed your list and ranked the words in order of importance, look at both your List of 100 Dreams and your Dream Themes one last time. To finalize your Values, ask yourself these questions about your ranked list:

- Did I miss anything?
- Is there any overlap?
- Do any of these words make more sense as part of a phrase?

- Can any of these words be combined to create a single value that captures my intent?
- Am I passionate about them?
- Are they easy to understand?
- Can I memorize them?
- Do I have too many?

Keep in mind that too many Values can dilute their meaning and make them more difficult to remember. Try to bring your list all the way down to five to seven.

Before finalizing these Values, write them on a sticky note or print them out on paper. Post these words or phrases where you'll see them often; keep them visible for a few days to make sure they really feel right before you commit.

Once you've put your Values into words by getting to the root of who you are and what matters most, it's unlikely they'll change drastically over the years. They'll be pretty steadfast and serve as the compass to guide your decisions. It's also possible that major life changes and transitions could cause a shift in your Values, and that's perfectly normal, too. If you sense that your Values no longer have the same meaning for you, revisit this exercise and refine your list.

• • •

Your Values are so much more than a collection of nice words. Now that you've articulated your Values, use them as your compass as you embark on your path toward achieving your Vision for the future. Keep them visible, even if that simply means jotting them on a sticky note that you post in your workspace. When you're reminded of your

Values, you're more likely to make decisions that align with who you are and what matters most to you.

HOW TO LIVE YOUR VISION AND VALUES

Now that you've clarified your Vision for the future and defined your personal Values, you may be wondering what exactly you're supposed to *do* with them. What does it actually look like to *live* your Vision and Values? How do you translate these ideas and words to the pages of your calendar and hours of your life?

You're certainly not alone in your curiosity about next steps. So often whenever we create something like a mission statement or our Vision and Values, we assume the next step is action.

Your next step now is less about *doing* and more about *being*.

When it comes to defining your Vision and Values, the power is in the process. The *doing* already happened as you captured your Vision and created your list of Values. Now it's time for *being*. And, you can do that by *being* your most authentic self and using your Vision and Values as a compass through each day and with each decision.

One of the biggest mistakes we can make after articulating our Vision and Values is to tuck the work we just did in a drawer and never look at it again. Instead, keep your Vision and Values top of mind—whether by posting them on your mirror, as a background on your phone, or somewhere else—so you can use them to drive your days.

Since your Values should be a relatively short list, challenge yourself to memorize them. Start by posting them somewhere you'll see them often, like your desk, your fridge, or the front cover of your planner.

Make a Vision and Values Brainstorm List

I hope you're feeling energized and excited to begin living your Vision and Values. But, how exactly do you translate words like *legacy*, *curiosity*, or *loyalty* into items on your to-do list? A Vision and Values Brainstorm List is a great place to start.

Begin this brainstorm by gathering your Vision notes and your list of Values.

Start with your Vision. What are the actions you can take in the next year, quarter, month, week, or day that will get you one step closer to making your Vision a reality? Write those actions down in a brainstorm list. This list is your inspiration for the next steps you can take to make your Vision a reality.

Next, grab your list of Values and start with the first value on your list. Make a list of at least five activities that represent that value to you. These actions should be things you can reasonably experience or complete in the near future. While it's OK to be a little aspirational, they should also be achievable.

Work your way down your Values list and continue building your list of actions that represent each value. If one of your Values is family, what are five actions you can take that will help you live that value today, tomorrow, or next week? If one of your Values is connection, honesty, courage, or faith, what are five actions you can take in the near future that exemplify that value? Chances are, you won't be able to stop at five!

Once you've created your Vision and Values brainstorm lists, keep them handy so you can refer back to them later. When you plan your week, ask yourself whether your Values are represented on your calendar. If yes, awesome! If not, consider making some changes that will enable you to proactively live each of your Values in some way.

TIME MANAGEMENT BEGINS WITH VISION AND VALUES

Now, you might be incredibly excited to have established a clear set of Vision and Values that will guide your Purpose—but you might also be wondering how these parts of your identity are going to come into play as we learn more about time management. I've got you covered.

Imagine a funnel, or an upside-down triangle that's big at the top and gets narrower at the bottom. Your *Vision* and *Values* are at the top; they represent who you are, and what's most important to you.

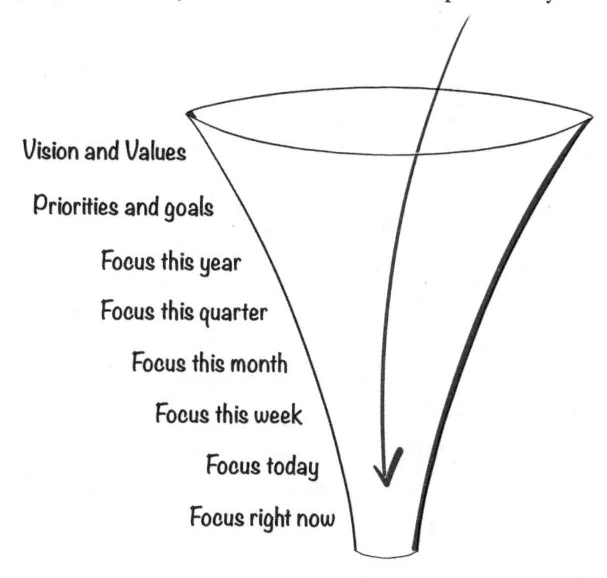

Your Values influence the next level down, your *priorities and goals.*

Your priorities and goals influence the next level down, which includes *what you need to do this year in order to achieve those goals.*

What you need to do this year determines *what you need to do this quarter.*

What you need to do this quarter affects *how you spend your time this month.*

What you need to accomplish this month affects *what you need to knock out this week.*

What you need to achieve this week determines *how you should spend today.*

And, at the very bottom of the funnel is the smallest point. What you need to do today affects *what you need to do right now.*

This is exactly why we don't begin a conversation about effective time management by discussing planners, calendars, and organizing tips. As much as I love those parts of time management, that's just not the best place to begin. Without a Vision for the future and Values to light the way, your time management isn't Purpose-driven—and time management without Purpose is reactive. That kind of time management looks like putting out one fire after another, giving the squeaky wheel the grease, and living from one day to the next. That's not sustainable or intentional, and it doesn't set you up to use your time or your gifts to their fullest.

I believe that you have gifts and strengths that the world needs. And if you're reading this book, you've got the drive to master time management.

If you stay focused and implement the time management essentials we will work through in this book, you will become Purpose-driven and unstoppable—as long as your Vision and Values guide the way.

ESSENTIAL TAKEAWAYS

At the end of each chapter, you'll find Essential Takeaways. These are the most important points you'll need to remember as you build your personal time management strategy using a layered approach that starts with identifying what matters most. In this chapter, the Essential Takeaways are:

- Effective time management begins with articulating your life's Purpose. Two time management tools that will help you articulate your life's Purpose are your Vision and your Values.
- Your Vision is your mental picture of what you want your future to look like. Having a Vision guides your decisions and gives you hope.
- Your Values are a collection of five to seven words that represent what matters most to you in life. They serve as guiding principles in your decision-making, including decisions about how you spend your time.
- The key to living your Vision and Values is keeping them visible and top of mind; connecting them with relevant, achievable actions; and constantly striving to be your most authentic self.

When Everything Feels Important

"It's out of control," a client shared with me, referring to her inbox. She explained that so many hours of her workday, evenings, and weekends were spent navigating her swamp of an inbox. She could never find anything she needed and was constantly missing deadlines. When her colleagues didn't get a response via email, they followed up with a Slack message. When they didn't hear from her on Slack, they checked in with a quick text. Soon, she was swimming in communications on three different channels and feeling completely overwhelmed.

Using a classic coaching question, I asked her to tell me what she'd tried so far to regain control over her mess of messages. She started by explaining how she organized her emails with a labeling system.

"Well first, there's Priority. That one's yellow. Then there's *High* Priority. That one's orange. Read Later is for things I want to read later. That one's blue. There's also aToday, which is a different shade of yellow."

I interrupted her. "I'm sorry. Did you say 'aToday'? Like 'today' with the letter *a* in front of it?"

"Yes, exactly. aToday. That's for things that need a response today. I added a lowercase *a* so the category shows up first on my list. I also have zUrgent."

"zUrgent? Tell me more about that," I responded.

"zUrgent is for the highest priority, most urgent emails. That one's purple. But there's also regular Urgent, which is red. Regular Urgent is less urgent than zUrgent, and I added a lowercase *z* to Urgent so it would show up at the bottom of my list. That way I know that aToday is at the top and zUrgent is at the bottom!"

I paused to take it all in. As a time management coach, I'm accustomed to helping clients find ways to spend less time on email and more time making an impact. This client, however, didn't have an email problem. Or, I should say, her inbox wasn't her primary problem. Instead, her overflowing inbox was a symptom of a much larger issue.

Every message, request, report, survey, announcement, newsletter, memo, white paper, and sale alert that hit her inbox was considered a priority. And there were so many competing priorities and levels of urgency that she began using a lowercase *a* and a lowercase *z* in front of words to manufacture a hierarchy. Her inbox was a mess because her priorities were a mess. So instead of sharing email management hacks or sorting tips that would get her to "Inbox Zero," we attacked the real problem. We clarified her priorities.

When you're running a business, leading a team, or shouldering any type of responsibility, especially when you care deeply about what you're doing, it's easy to fall into the trap of believing that every task, to-do, project, or request is of equal importance. But, as organizational consultant and author Patrick Lencioni said, "When everything is important, nothing is." Vilfredo Pareto likely would have agreed.

THE 80/20 RULE

Let's travel back to the early 1900s. Economist Vilfredo Pareto was at the University of Lausanne in Switzerland studying the distribution of wealth across populations. Using land ownership as a signifier of wealth, Pareto found that 80 percent of Italy's land was owned by 20 percent of its population. Curious about the distribution of land ownership and wealth in other countries, he continued his research and found similar results. Over and over again, Pareto found this 80:20 ratio to be consistent across countries regardless of the population, geography, or key industries.

Fast-forward to 1941 when Joseph Juran, a Romanian-born American engineer, discovered Pareto's work. Juran's focus on quality management in mechanical engineering inspired him to apply Pareto's research to manufacturing quality issues. The 80:20 ratio appeared again, this time describing the cause and effect of manufacturing mistakes.

Juran found that 80 percent of errors, issues, and problems are a result of 20 percent of causes. Juran's continuation of Pareto's work established what we now know as the Pareto principle, Pareto's principle, or the 80/20 rule.

Pareto Principle

80% of your outputs come from 20% of your inputs.

The Pareto principle states that for many outcomes, roughly 80 percent of the outputs come from 20 percent of the inputs.

If you look closely, you'll find that the Pareto principle is present in a multitude of places, spaces, and situations.

In business, it typically follows that 80 percent of a company's revenue comes from 20 percent of its products, services, or clients. When zooming in specifically on managing client relationships, it's likely that 20 percent of your clients require 80 percent of your time and attention. In a company's content marketing plan, it's likely that 20 percent of the content created—whether for blog posts, podcasts, videos, or events—is responsible for 80 percent of new leads generated. The Pareto principle shows up in our homes, as well. If I were to open your closet, it's likely that you reach for 20 percent of your clothes 80 percent of the time. In your kitchen, I'll bet you use 20 percent of your kitchen tools 80 percent of the time. You can probably even picture the exact pots and pans, spatulas, and bowls in that 20 percent.

So, what does this mean for us in terms of time management? Simply put, some activities are more important than others since they give us more bang for our buck, more results for our time, and more return on investment (ROI) for our efforts. It's up to us to determine what those 20 percent activities are though. Start paying attention to which items on your to-do list give you the most impactful results—those are likely part of your 20 percent.

Knowing this information is incredibly important. For example, when you know which client relationships are most valuable, which marketing activities are most profitable, and which meetings are most useful, you're able to prioritize those activities and move them to the top of your to-do list to ensure you're spending your time where it really counts.

UNDERSTANDING PRIORITIES

The most common struggles I encounter as a time management coach typically relate in some way to unclear priorities, or a misunderstanding of priorities altogether:

> "I need to get my priorities in order."
>
> "I need to prioritize better."
>
> "My priorities are all over the place."

Usually, priority-induced frustration takes a few different forms. In some cases, it's having trouble deciding how to spend your time in the moment, like trying to figure out what to do first or next. Instead of moving forward and choosing how to spend your time with intention, your head spins trying to decide which of your projects to work on next. Many times, that feeling of being overwhelmed can be paralyzing and then nothing of substance gets done.

Frustration about priorities can sometimes be a result of *knowing* what's most important, but instead of taking action, you procrastinate and avoid the task at hand. You know what you *should* be doing, but getting started feels intimidating or uncomfortable—like standing at the base of a mountain, looking up to the peak, and feeling your stomach drop anticipating the arduous climb ahead.

Another common priority problem is feeling pulled in many different directions. Everything feels equally important, so deciding what to do feels impossible. How can you choose what to do when *everything* needs to be done, and it all needs to be done *now*?

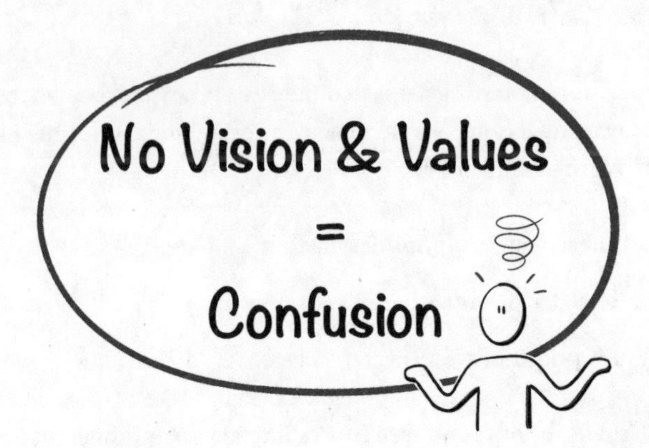

When there's no clear Vision or Values guiding your decisions, deciding what to do in any given moment becomes a reactive game. Priorities driven by our Vision and Values help us make confident decisions about how to spend our time.

• • •

When I learned the history of the word *priority*, it blew my mind. It might surprise you, too, to learn that the idea of having multiple priorities is a fairly new concept. The word *priority* comes from the Latin *prioritas,* meaning "first in rank, order, or dignity." Think about that. There can only be *one* first thing. *One*. One first person in line. One first item on the agenda. Just *one*.

The word *priorities* didn't begin to appear in print until the 1940s. Pluralizing the word *priority* into *priorities* attempts to make multiple things the first thing, which we can agree is impossible. It is impossible to have multiple first things. Yet we see companies setting dozens of quarterly priorities, and nonprofits creating pages-long donor priority lists. We also see employees and entrepreneurs struggling to identify the *real* "first thing" in a sea of competing "first things."

Now you may be wondering, how can we adapt our understanding of the original meaning of *priority* to the modern world we live in? The truth is, as much as we'd love to focus our time and attention on just *one* thing, as the word *priority* intended, that's not our reality anymore. In any one job, we're wearing a lot of hats, and in our personal lives, we usually have multiple goals to hit and a long list of things to do.

So, how many priorities is too many? While this answer will be unique to you, your life, and your responsibilities, I believe three to four priorities is manageable within different areas or categories of life. Obviously, the fewer the better, but more than four and their importance becomes diluted. That being said, to be the most successful when having multiple priorities, even as few as four, ranking them in order of importance is absolutely critical.

Types of Priorities

If the thought of choosing only three to four priorities across all of the roles and responsibilities in your life feels daunting or even impossible, have no fear. It's completely logical to have unique priorities for different areas of your life, as well as priorities for specific periods of time.

Priorities can be divided into two main categories: strategic (or big-picture) priorities and tactical (or day-to-day) priorities.

Strategic Priorities	Day-to-Day Priorities
• What's most important in a broad sense of your life or business • Usually kept in place for longer periods of time: monthly, quarterly, annually, or even longer	• Task-oriented priorities that direct how you spend your time and move you closer to your vision

Strategic Priorities

Strategic or big-picture priorities describe what's most important in a broad sense of your life or business. They are the overarching themes, categories, or "buckets" of activities that move you closer to making your Vision a reality. If your Vision includes retiring early, one of your strategic priorities will likely be financial security. If your Vision includes seeing the world, one of your strategic priorities will likely be travel. Strategic priorities are usually kept in place for longer periods of time: monthly, quarterly, annually, or even longer.

When choosing strategic priorities for different areas of your life, it's important to first identify what those different areas are. Start by making a list of the different roles and responsibilities you have in life. Your roles represent who you are, often in relationship to others. Examples of roles include parent, daughter, volunteer, supervisor, colleague, and neighbor. Your responsibilities describe the different areas or categories of your life. For many, health and wellness, spirituality, finances, parenting, relationships, career/business, and hobbies make the list.

Once you've made your list of roles and responsibilities, identify the three to four most important activities or tactics within each role or responsibility. Remember the Pareto principle and identify the most impactful activities that propel you forward in each area.

For example, if one of the most important areas of your life includes health and wellness, your list of health and wellness priorities might look like this:

1. Good nutrition
2. Exercise
3. Meditation

You've identified these three things as the highest Value activities in the area of health and wellness, and you've decided that eating healthy foods will give you the most ROI—even if you're unable to exercise or meditate with your available time.

Within your business, your collection of strategic and tactical priorities will likely be a bit more complex based on the size and structure of your business. Different departments, divisions, or teams within your business may have their own sets of priorities that move them closer to reaching company goals. However, I've found that maintaining three to four strategic business priorities for at least a quarter or the full year gives your team, regardless of your business size, a shared set of priorities to rally around. When your team is confused about what's most important, it inevitably leads to wasted time, wasted resources, and lost opportunities. When it comes to priorities, less is definitely more.

Tactical Priorities

While your strategic priorities in your business, health, or relationships may be steadfast for longer periods of time, the most important thing to do in each area can change from month to month and from minute to minute. Tactical, or day-to-day, priorities are the task-oriented priorities that direct how you spend your time. Like many things in life, prioritization is a constant practice. And, in order to truly spend time on what matters most, we've got to be ruthless about sifting through the sand, doing the next right thing, and letting the rest go. Ruthless prioritization.

CHOOSE YOUR TOP 3

So now that we understand priorities (and the two different types of priorities), it's time for some ruthless prioritization skills, and one of my favorites is to choose your Weekly Top 3 and Daily Top 3.

At the beginning of each week, before you even start your workday on Monday, set aside 15–30 minutes to scan the week and month ahead and assess any upcoming deadlines or project milestones. Then, ask yourself: What are the Top 3 things I must do *this week* in order to stay on track?

Keep in mind that these are not the *only* three things you'll do in the week ahead. Instead, they are the three *most important things* you will do in the week ahead. By identifying those three things at the onset of the week, you're more likely to carve out time for each and end your week feeling accomplished. Plus, when requests for your time pop up, you'll be able to better provide availability and set expectations because you've already carved out time to do your most important work.

Your next step after choosing your Weekly Top 3 is to choose your Daily Top 3. Ask yourself, What are the Top 3 things I must do *today* in order to stay on track? Just like defining your Weekly Top 3 enables you to carve out time during the week ahead for your most important work, choosing your Daily Top 3 requires you to choose the most important high-impact tasks of the day. Make sure to begin each day by identifying your Daily Top 3 because doing so ensures you're not leaving your day to chance and you're beginning your day in proactive mode rather than reactive mode. You're deciding how your day will go, instead of letting your day run you.

It's important to note that three isn't a magic number. However, three is typically a manageable number of important tasks to complete in the course of a single day. Here's why: A typical eight-hour workday can be divided into four two-hour blocks. Our brains are only able to engage in deep concentration for 90 minutes to two hours before we become fatigued, less productive, and more prone to error. If you take an hour break for lunch and add in a few small breaks throughout the day, you're left with approximately three two-hour focus blocks. If you're a manager or your work includes lots of meetings or phone calls, then you likely have even fewer blocks of focus time available. Making a Daily Top 3 is typically just the right amount of high-impact tasks to prioritize in a single workday!

That being said, it's important to call out that during some seasons of life, you may need to downsize your Daily Top 3. A Daily Top 2 or even a Top 1 is nothing to be ashamed of.

When the world shut down in March 2020 in response to Covid-19, I suddenly found myself running my time management coaching business while taking care of my 15-month-old little girl. My husband, Scott, had been assigned to a worksite several hours from our home, so I was home alone continuing to serve clients while making snacks and corralling a newly mobile toddler.

In the beginning, I tried to maintain my Daily Top 3. Then, I bumped it down to a Daily Top 2. Finally, after struggling to balance running my business with caring for my little girl, I accepted that I was squarely in a season of choosing a Daily Top 1. Ruthless prioritization was the name of the game. Every morning, I asked myself, "What is the single most important thing I must do today in order to keep my business moving forward?"

When you're forced to choose the most important, most impactful activity, whether it's sending client invoices or making five sales calls, it's amazing what you're able to accomplish with limited time and resources.

HOW TO CHOOSE YOUR PRIORITIES

Now that you know that strategic priorities represent what's most important in a broad sense, and tactical priorities are the day-to-day activities that move you closer to your Vision, how exactly do you go about *choosing* your priorities in life and work? This is when your Vision for the future and your Values really shine.

Recall from Chapter 1 that your Vision is what you hope your future will look like. Your Values are the principles that guide your decisions and reflect what's most important to you.

When choosing priorities for life, start by reviewing your Vision. What do you want your life to look like 5 or 10 years from now? Then, boil your Vision down into three to four overarching themes. What do you need to focus on in the next quarter or the next year to move one step closer to making your Vision a reality?

The same process can be applied to selecting your business priorities. What is your business's Vision and Values? Start by reviewing your Vision and reflecting upon your company's Values. Then, identify the three to four overarching themes or areas of focus for the next quarter or year that will get you one step closer to making your Vision a reality.

Whether you're identifying your priorities in your personal life or for your business, starting with your Vision and Values will always steer you in the right direction.

HOW TO DECIDE WHAT TO DO FIRST WHEN EVERYTHING FEELS IMPORTANT

If you're reading this chapter on priorities from a place of being overwhelmed, I've got you covered. It's not unusual for a busy professional to have 300 to 400 outstanding tasks and to-dos at any given moment. So if you're feeling crushed by the weight of your to-do list, you're not alone. When there are so many different things that we *could* do, it makes defining what we *should* do first or next feel impossible. That's where Dwight D. Eisenhower, thirty-fourth president of the United States, comes in.

By all accounts, President Eisenhower was a productive guy. He rose through the ranks of the US Army to become a five-star general. He founded NASA, signed the Civil Rights Act of 1957, and much more. His secret to getting so much accomplished is what we now call the Eisenhower Matrix.

The Eisenhower Matrix

The Eisenhower Matrix, sometimes called the Eisenhower Decision Matrix, the Eisenhower Box, or the Eisenhower Method, is an extremely popular and effective time management strategy used by highly effective people to get their most important work done. It's a method for categorizing and prioritizing the items on your to-do list according to their urgency and importance.

The Eisenhower Matrix is ideal to use when you're feeling overwhelmed, you're not sure where to start, or you find yourself missing deadlines.

It starts with a box containing four quadrants.

	Urgent	Not Urgent
Important	Tasks that are both urgent and important	Tasks that are important, but not urgent
Not Important	Tasks that are urgent, but not important	Tasks that are neither urgent, nor important

When everything feels important, and you're not sure where to start, begin by sorting your tasks into each quadrant. Then, once you've sorted your tasks based on urgency and importance, here are your next steps:

- **Top Left Quadrant: Urgent and Important.** The more urgent and important something is, the higher it should be on your list for the day. Examples typically include mission-critical, deadline-based tasks for your most important projects.

Action: DO these first.

- **Top Right Quadrant: Important, but Not Urgent.** Items in this quadrant are usually important activities such as personal development, long-term planning, or other activities without a set or immediate deadline. In your personal life, top right activities could include exercise or meditation. Since these nonurgent, but important items can easily be put on the back burner and occasionally forgotten, it's important to schedule these activities on your calendar. Then, do your best to stick to your schedule.

  Action: DEFER these by scheduling time for them.

- **Bottom Left Quadrant: Urgent, but Not Important.** This is when knowing your Vision and your Values is especially critical because you've got to have some kind of filter so you can decide what's important and what's not. Something that pops up and is urgent but unimportant to your Vision and Values is the ideal activity to delegate to someone else. If you don't have someone to delegate your bottom left tasks to, look for opportunities to automate these tasks so you're not stuck tackling them in the future. There are a number of programs available to incorporate automation into your workflows. In summary, if something falls in this category, delegate it if you can and make it more efficient if you can't.

  Action: DELEGATE these tasks.

- **Bottom Right Quadrant: Not Urgent, Not Important.** Basically, what's the point? These tasks look like bad habits, such as scrolling social media without a specific reason in mind, or tasks that don't align with your Vision and Values. Often, things we've said yes to out of obligation fall into this category. If something falls in this quadrant, we cut it.

  Action: DELETE these tasks and move on.

Writer Mark Twain said, "The secret of getting ahead is getting started." Often, just getting started is the hardest part of time management and productivity. It's tough to know what to do first when you're feeling overwhelmed. But, using the Eisenhower Matrix can help you identify what items on your to-do list should stay, what you should do first, and which you should cut by delegating or eliminating them altogether. This enables you to free up more time to focus on what matters most.

President Eisenhower might have been a very accomplished individual, but the Eisenhower Matrix is a time management technique anyone can use to clarify their tactical priorities when feeling overwhelmed.

PURPOSE-DRIVEN PRIORITIES

When you use your Vision for the future and your Values to define your strategic and tactical priorities, you're able to step into each day with confidence, make decisions with clarity, and live with intention. Anytime your priorities begin to feel murky, revisit your Vision and Values to reconnect your priorities to your Purpose. When overwhelmed, rely on the Eisenhower Matrix to reveal what's urgent and important. With this perspective on Purpose-driven priorities, you're armed with exactly what you need to avoid the most common productivity pitfalls.

ESSENTIAL TAKEAWAYS

- The Pareto principle states that for many outcomes, 80 percent of the outputs are a result of 20 percent of the inputs. Applied to time management, this tells us that some tasks, projects, or to-dos are more impactful than others, and therefore more worthy of our limited time.
- Priorities, like your Vision and Values, guide your decision-making about how to spend your time. Priorities can be strategic and span months, quarters, or years. They can also be tactical and guide your short-term time allocation for a week, a day, or even an hour.
- The Eisenhower Matrix is a framework for prioritizing your current tasks. By organizing your activities based on levels of urgency and importance, you can easily decide your next action, schedule your upcoming work, identify opportunities to delegate, and eliminate some things altogether.

Productivity Pitfalls to Watch Out For

When I was a little girl, one of my favorite things to do was play with my dad's old Atari video game set. If you're not familiar, Atari was a video computer system that came before the original Nintendo in the 1980s. The controller was literally just a joystick with a single red button. Compared to the ultra-realistic video games of today, Atari games were basically dots, lines, and stick figures. If you can picture the original Pac-Man, you're on the right track.

In one of my favorite games, you helped a little man run through the jungle and collect treasures. Push the joystick left or right to make him run. Press the red button to make him jump. Pretty simple. The little man had to grab swinging vines to cross tar pits; hop on crocodile heads to traverse water holes; jump over rattlesnakes, scorpions, and fire; and avoid a multitude of obstacles to collect treasures before time ran out.

The game was called *Pitfall!* and the little man, named Pitfall Harry, just couldn't catch a break. He was constantly jumping, dodging, avoiding, and overcoming obstacles to achieve his goal. Plus, he was always running full speed and racing to beat the clock.

Sometimes during my workday, I feel a little like Pitfall Harry. Dodging distractions in the form of emails, Slack messages, text messages, Voxer messages, and even the occasional phone call. Plus, back-to-back-to-back Zoom meetings. And, trying to stay focused and avoid time wasters like checking TikTok, Instagram, or my kids' preschool photo app to see if any new snapshots have been uploaded in the last 20 minutes. At the end of some days, my eyes have glazed over and my brain feels fried.

We may not be jumping on crocodile heads and crossing swamps, but navigating low-value requests for our time, getting to Inbox Zero, meeting deadlines, planning meals, remembering birthdays, signing permission slips, and making time for #allthethings can be pretty exhausting.

Something that can make the jungle of distraction feel just a little more manageable is being aware of the productivity pitfalls that could work for you—but could also work against you. Being aware of how these seemingly positive tools and tactics could actually turn into a negative is crucial when it comes to being productive. When you know the ins and outs of these pitfalls, you can spot them before they give you trouble. So, let's get to know three of the most common productivity pitfalls a little better.

PITFALL 1: PARKINSON'S LAW

"I'm really good under pressure."

"If you give me a deadline, I can make it happen."

If you've ever found yourself uttering either of those sentences before, then you've encountered Parkinson's Law.

Parkinson's Law states that work expands to fill the time allotted. And, this pitfall explains why waiting until the last minute before a deadline can sometimes produce a faster turnaround than starting the same project with more than enough time to spare. It also explains why we can easily fall into the bad habit of letting our work creep into other areas of our lives. The boundaries between work and downtime are very blurry and, in many cases, invisible.

In spring 2020, the world experienced an unprecedented shift to remote work in response to the Covid-19 pandemic. Suddenly, we found ourselves working from our kitchen tables, spare bedrooms, sofa, and anywhere we could find a decent enough background to host a Zoom meeting. Without clear policies in place to support a healthy work-from-home environment (and navigating so many unknowns in the world), employees quickly began to struggle with burnout. The boundaries between work and home were gone, and many of us couldn't tell if we were working from home or homing from work.

Work expands to fill the time allotted. So, when our workday doesn't have a clear end, work inevitably spills over into all aspects of our day. It takes over our thoughts when we're trying to engage with family at dinner. It takes over our nights when we lie in bed thinking about an upcoming project instead of getting a good night's rest. It takes over our weekends when we try to play catch-up before running errands and getting ready for a new workweek.

Without boundaries in place, we get less rest and enjoy less leisure time. We take fewer vacation days and neglect our relationships. We burn out. That's why it's critical we create our own healthy boundaries in the form of clear workday start and stop times—and commit to sticking to them.

Parkinson's Law applies not just to your workday, but to your individual projects, as well. When you have an assignment without a concrete deadline, you could literally continue working on it until the end of time. With no deadline, there's always one more thing that could be edited, adjusted, tweaked, reviewed, or changed. You can adjust font size, swap the colors, add an image, add another image, and continue toiling away in the impossible pursuit of perfection.

When you have a clear deadline to work against, Parkinson's Law is your friend. You have a clear boundary and a set end time; work can only take up the space available. You're forced to make decisions. You're forced to take action. You're forced to just get it done. In addition to setting clear boundaries around your workday, using time blocking (see Chapter 4) to create boundaries within your day is an effective way to use Parkinson's Law to your advantage.

In the end, this pitfall can work for or against you depending on the boundaries you create. Knowing that work expands without boundaries, you can create intentional start and stop times and keep your work where it belongs.

PITFALL 2: THE PLANNING FALLACY

Have you ever been frustrated when a task on your to-do list took so much longer than you expected? You thought those edits would only take you about 30 minutes, and two hours later, you're still chugging away, wide-eyed and weary staring at your computer.

One of my all-star time management clients, Corinn, was flustered and frustrated when we began working together. She consistently worked nights and weekends and was missing out on quality time with her husband and baby girl. After asking her what techniques she'd tried so far to manage her time during her busy workdays, she shared that she used time blocking to schedule her tasks in her calendar each week.

At face value, this sounded great! On Monday mornings, she'd look ahead and fill her entire week with time blocks to represent all of the tasks to be completed by the end of the week. Every minute had a purpose, and every day had a plan. Sounds like a dream, right?

Here's where it all fell apart. On Monday morning, the first task on her list took 30 minutes longer than the estimated time block on her calendar. She then had to push the next time block further down in the day. Then the next time block had to be pushed back, and so on and so on until she was working late into the evening and on weekends to cross everything off her list, fulfill obligations to her team, and meet deadlines for her department. She was exhausted, and for good reason. She realized that she was "meticulously underestimating" what she could accomplish and how long it would take her every single day.

If Corinn's meticulously underestimated schedule sounds familiar, you're not alone. Chronic underestimation is the Planning Fallacy in action.

The Planning Fallacy describes our tendency to underestimate how much time it will take us to complete a task. I actually find the Planning Fallacy to be a very comforting productivity pitfall because it's proof that this is something we *all* struggle with.

Fortunately, when you're aware of the Planning Fallacy, you can adjust your estimations, give yourself buffer time, and create more accurate time blocks. By using the Planning Fallacy to your advantage, you can set achievable deadlines and realistic expectations for yourself and others.

By the way, after Corinn began keeping the Planning Fallacy in mind while mapping out her weeks, she accomplished more than anyone ever had in her role and was dubbed "the most productive person in the office" by her coworkers. And through the work we'll do together in this book, that's possible for you, too.

PITFALL 3: PROCRASTINATION

Imagine a scale. Not the kind you step on in the bathroom, but a balance scale like the scales of justice. This scale has a little basket or bucket on each side that tips toward the heavier side.

Now, imagine that this scale is your Taking Action scale. One bucket is labeled "Self-Control and Motivation" and the other bucket is "Negative Factors."

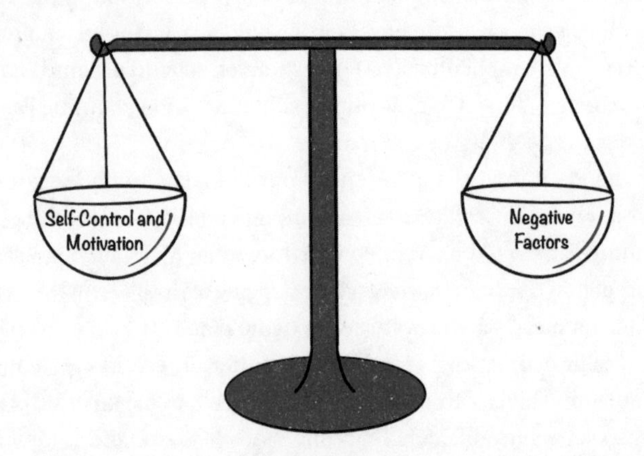

Let's take a closer look at the true meaning of self-control and how it impacts our behavior. Merriam-Webster defines self-control as "restraint exercised over one's own impulses, emotions, or desires." It's your ability to control yourself. Motivation is the reason why we act or behave in a certain way.

Negative factors include anxiety, fear of failure, unpleasantness of the task, exhaustion, boredom, and others. Negative factors are all the reasons why we *don't* want to do something.

If your self-control and motivation are stronger than the negative factors, you're more likely to follow through and take action. But if the negative factors outweigh your self-control and motivation, you're more likely to avoid the task, letting procrastination win.

According to Merriam-Webster, procrastination is "to put off intentionally the doing of something that should be done." Mountains of research, books, articles, and podcast episodes have been dedicated to the all-too-common pitfall of procrastination, but there are three things you should know about procrastination and how it affects your time management.

1. Everybody Procrastinates

Studies have found that 95 percent of us procrastinate to some degree.[1] If you're reading this and you're in the 5 percent that never procrastinates, please reach out to me directly so I can interview you for an upcoming episode of my podcast, *It's About Time.*

If you procrastinate, clearly these statistics prove you're not alone. As someone who is definitely in that 95 percent, I know procrastination is often accompanied by shame and negative self-talk. We know we're putting something off, which can give us a small feeling of relief. But we also feel guilt and shame because we're not doing what we know we're supposed to be doing. Sometimes you start to believe that other people are better than you because they don't procrastinate like you do. You may believe you're falling behind and will never catch up because you can't do things when you need to.

Let me repeat: You are not alone. Procrastination is totally normal.

2. Procrastination Isn't Laziness

One of the aspects of procrastination that can cause shame is believing procrastination means we're inherently lazy. Let's look at procrastination and laziness separately.

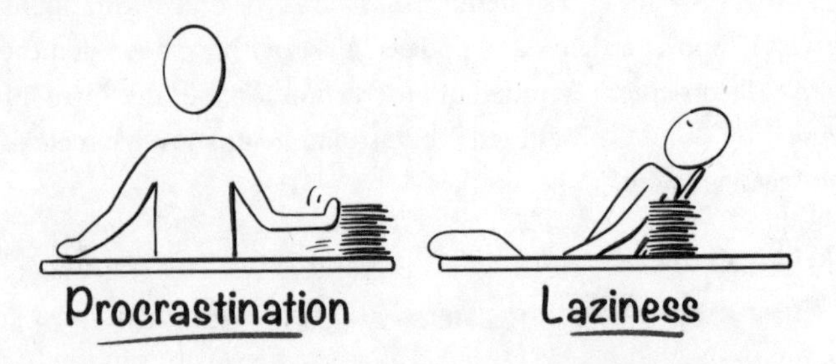

Procrastination is choosing to put something off or do something else instead of that "something." Procrastination is an action.

Laziness, on the other hand, is an unwillingness to put in the effort to do something. This simplifies the concept of laziness, but it's more of a feeling.

Procrastination is an action. Laziness is a feeling.

3. Procrastination Has Benefits

Although we can be hard on ourselves for procrastination, there are actually some benefits to it. Let's look at three of them.

Procrastination Benefit 1: You Can Work Quicker

When you put something off until the last minute, Parkinson's Law kicks in. If you give yourself two weeks to assemble a report, it'll probably take you the full two weeks. If you give yourself two hours to knock out the same report because you have a meeting with your boss in two hours, you'll probably find a way to get it done in those two hours.

When you wait until the last minute, you typically get a boost of adrenaline, focus, work quickly, and lower your expectations. Perfectionism tends to go out the window because you've got to get it done. If you've ever said, "I totally thrive under pressure," then you know exactly what this feels like.

Procrastination Benefit 2: You Can Make Better Decisions

Sometimes in the process of procrastinating, you uncover new information, think about something in a new light, or shift your priorities. You may have an opportunity to calm down and regain your composure instead of making an irrational, emotional response. Additionally, when we allow information to marinate in our subconscious mind, our brains start solving problems and making connections in the background while we're focused on other things. This is why we often have great ideas in the shower or while taking a walk. You know the advice to "sleep on it" before making a big decision? That's actually a great example of when procrastination is a good thing.

Procrastination Benefit 3: You Can Get Other Things Done

Back when I was schlepping media ethics and communications law textbooks under stately oaks and broad magnolias as an undergraduate at LSU, my can't-miss first step to begin studying for finals wasn't to crack open my textbook or review my class notes. Instead, I began by cleaning my apartment from top to bottom. Vacuuming, washing the windows, cleaning the bathtubs, and removing every speck of dust was on my to-do list. Then, after I'd thoroughly cleaned the apartment, I'd pack up and head to the library feeling ready to tackle test prep.

Productive procrastination—sometimes called purposeful procrastination, positive procrastination, or intentional delay—can be a very healthy part of the creative process. Just like procrastination can help you make better decisions, great ideas can come from idle time or time spent doing low-impact tasks. In a way you're doing two things at once, accomplishing a low-impact task while mentally preparing for a high-focus task.

When it comes to procrastination, it's important to remember that you're not alone and there are some benefits to putting things off. However, when procrastination is unchecked, it can put a big damper on your productivity. Fortunately, when you spot procrastination and recognize that your self-control and motivation don't beat out the negative factors, you can balance the scales and take action using proven time management strategies.

ESSENTIAL TAKEAWAYS

- Parkinson's Law states that work expands to fill the time allotted. If we don't define a clear end time, we could keep working forever. Parkinson's Law also explains why we tend to work faster as a deadline looms. By using the strategy of time blocking, you can combat Parkinson's Law by creating boundaries for your work.
- The Planning Fallacy describes our tendency to underestimate how much time it will take to complete a task. Combat the Planning Fallacy by adding extra time to your time blocks.
- Everyone procrastinates from time to time. Procrastination and laziness are not the same thing, and not all procrastination is bad. Sometimes it leads to better decision-making and helps you move past perfectionism and actually get things done.

CHAPTER

4

Time Management Tactics That Save the Day

During the late 1880s, the leaders of a European military organization wanted to make life easier for their soldiers. They wanted their men to have the tools necessary to open canned food, repair and maintain their rifles, and be better prepared for the situations they might encounter on the front lines. But instead of issuing each soldier a toolbox filled with any instrument they could possibly need, the leaders pursued a more streamlined approach.

The soldiers needed a collection of tools they could easily transport, but those tools needed to be compact and light enough to avoid substantially increasing the weight of the soldier's load. The soldier's knife, a pocket-sized multipurpose tool, was born. The earliest soldier's knife included a blade, reamer, can opener, and screwdriver. Each instrument could swivel out of the handle and be pushed back into place. It weighed around 5 ounces (about the same as your smartphone). Today, the term "Swiss Army knife" is used to describe anything that's useful, multipurpose, and adaptable.

This chapter is your Swiss Army knife of time management tools: equipped with time blocking, task batching, and theme days. You can use these three strategies on their own or use them stacked or layered—in a multitude of combinations—to adapt to the different seasons of life.

SWISS ARMY KNIFE TOOL #1: TIME BLOCKING

When many people think about the US Congress, they envision lively debates, controversial votes, and elected officials speaking behind podiums in dark suits on C-SPAN. However, the real heroes of Capitol Hill, the ones who actually make everything happen, are staffers known as schedulers.

While all of the roles within a congressional office enable our government to function, without the scheduler, everything would fall apart. Seriously. The scheduler, you may be able to deduce based on the title, is responsible for managing the representative's schedule.

It's common for a scheduler to receive hundreds of requests for the official's time in the course of a week. Requests come from constituents, lobbyists, special interest groups, local elected officials, school groups, nonprofit organizations, and more. In addition to meeting requests, a member of Congress can receive dozens of speaking requests, invitations to receptions, dinners, fundraisers, ribbon cutting ceremonies, school functions, church fish fries, and more. Add in committee meetings and a vote schedule that can change at the drop of a hat, and it's easy to see why the scheduler has one of the most important and demanding jobs on the Hill. Schedulers make sure members are spending their time in the most impactful way possible, and that they're where they need to be when they need to be. The scheduler is a master of time orchestration.

So, what tools does the scheduler use to make the impossible possible? First up is time blocking. For members of Congress, every day is filled with intentional time blocks for meetings and downtime. Downtime, although limited, is critical to the schedule's success.

If you haven't already guessed, I was once a scheduler for a congressman. In my first week on the job, I learned the hard way that downtime is essential when I failed to include time blocks for bathroom breaks for my boss. Whoops.

What Is Time Blocking?

Time blocking is exactly what it sounds like: creating blocks in your schedule to represent how you will spend your time. If you're putting meetings and appointments into your calendar, you're already using time blocking to stay on schedule. However, as I learned as a scheduler that needed to carve out bathroom breaks for my boss, time blocking is for so much more than just meetings and appointments. It's like scheduling a meeting with yourself to accomplish a specific task.

Benefits of time blocking include combating Parkinson's Law and the Planning Fallacy as well as decreasing context switching, which means working more efficiently and accurately.

By creating a time block in your calendar for something on your to-do list, you're giving the task a set start time, and a set end time—directly combating Parkinson's Law. Work expands to fill the time allotted, remember? So, when you create a time block with a precise end time, work can only expand up until that end time. You're forced to make decisions within the time block that will squash perfectionism in favor of finishing the task at hand.

Using time blocks also combats the Planning Fallacy. Knowing that the Planning Fallacy exists and that we all struggle to accurately estimate how long things take, you can intentionally set aside more time than you think you may need. For example, if you decide that a report will likely take you 30 minutes to edit, give yourself 45 instead. Boom—you just beat the Planning Fallacy!

Time blocking also helps you design a more realistic schedule. Since there are only so many hours in the day, creating time blocks for to-do list tasks gives an accurate picture of what you can actually accomplish. If you've ever felt frustrated at the end of the day for only tackling 4 of 37 things on your to-do list, time blocking can show you it's unrealistic to expect to complete 37 things in a single day. The time just isn't there.

Context switching is typically thought of as multitasking or doing multiple tasks at the same time. Context switching, sometimes called task switching, is shifting focus between unrelated tasks—and time blocking helps combat this, too. Whenever we switch from one task to the next, part of our attention stays with the first task instead of fully focusing on the new task. This is called attention residue—when you switch to something new, you can't give all of your mental energy to the new task because some of your focus is still devoted to the previous one. Like it or not, your brain is trying to focus on two things at once, which means you're more likely to make mistakes.

Context switching results in more errors than focusing on one task at a time, and it can mean losing 40–80 percent of your productive time. It takes an average of 23 minutes to regain your focus every time you context switch because different parts of your brain are activated every time you switch.[1] If you've ever felt completely scatterbrained, frazzled, and fatigued from being pulled in a dozen different directions during the day, context switching is likely to blame.

When you use time blocking to schedule your day, each block becomes a commitment to a single task for a specific time frame. This cuts back on context switching and enables you to give as much of your mental energy and focus as possible to the task at hand. That means more accuracy and fewer errors to correct, plus you make more substantial progress than if you skipped around to a number of different tasks throughout the day.

Where to Keep Your Time Blocks

Now that you understand what time blocking is, let's start using this incredibly helpful tool. Since time blocking creates a visual representation of the time you'll spend on each activity in your day, a digital calendar or a paper planner with a vertical hour-by-hour layout is best.

If you're new to time blocking, start with a digital option like Google Calendar or Outlook. With a digital calendar, you can easily resize time blocks and drag and drop them if you need to reschedule. In a paper planner, rescheduling can quickly become messy with scratch outs, scribbles, or arrows as you're learning time blocking. Some people don't mind the scratch outs and scribbles, but most prefer a clean, easy-to-read schedule.

There's another benefit of time blocking with a digital option. You can review and update your time blocks from different media platforms including your computer, smartphone, or tablet. On the other hand, if you leave your paper planner at your desk, or God forbid, accidentally leave it behind after a coffee shop working session, you're lost.

How to Start Time Blocking

Once you've decided *where* you'll time block, getting started is simple. First, review your to-do list and choose a task to time block. Next, estimate how long that task will take you. Consider adding additional time to your estimate based on the Planning Fallacy. Even if you don't need the buffer time, you'll be glad you have it just in case. Then, create a block in your calendar to represent that task. Repeat with your remaining priority tasks for the day. And, remember, if you have a Weekly Top 3 or a Daily Top 3, create time blocks for those tasks first.

When it's time to begin your time-blocked activity, focus only on that task until the time block ends. That's it!

How to Create More Accurate Time Blocks

If you embark on your time blocking journey and find that even with additional buffer time, you're struggling to accurately estimate your time blocks, it's helpful to conduct a time study. For my time management clients who confess, "I just have *no* idea where my time is going!" conducting a one-week time study answers that question.

Similar to keeping a food journal in which you write down everything you eat for a specific period of time, a time study is a log of how you're spending your time for a designated period. It includes every detail of your day, from waking up and brushing your teeth to turning off the light before bedtime. It gives you a realistic picture of your day and can reveal how long things actually take you, when you're prone to wasting time, and opportunities to streamline your day.

How to Do a Time Study

To do a time study, start by deciding where you'll track your time. A spreadsheet, phone note, Google Doc, or notebook you can carry with you are all good options. Software like Clockify, Harvest, and Toggl Track makes time tracking simple, too. Then, every 15 to 30 minutes throughout the day, jot down a few notes about how you spent your time. The more detail you capture, the better. Be sure to make notes about how you're feeling during different times of the day, too. For example, "Zoom call with Stacy about the Rivers project. Felt tired before but energized after" is more useful than "Zoom call" or "work."

The ideal time frame for a time study is at least a week, and you'll want to be strategic about the week you decide to log. Aim to capture a "normal" seven-day period. For example, if you don't usually travel for work or attend conferences, don't do your time study while you're traveling or attending a conference. However, don't delay your time study waiting for the "perfect" week to appear. There's no such thing as a perfect representation of a typical workweek. Something almost always pops up. A doctor's appointment, a sick child, or some type of unexpected event is actually quite normal.

At the end of your time study, carve out at least 30 minutes to review your entries and see what you can learn about how you spend your time. Consider these questions:

- When during your week did you feel your best, or most energized?
- When did you feel your worst, or most fatigued or frustrated?
- Where are you wasting time?
- When are you context switching instead of staying focused on one task?
- How long did your priority tasks take you?
- How can you rearrange certain parts of your week to create more opportunities for uninterrupted focus time?

A time study can open your eyes to where your time is actually going. It can reveal what you're doing right, as well as opportunities for improvement, and you might be surprised by what you find. One of my clients struggled to find work-life balance. She assumed she was spending a disproportionate amount of time working, and as a result, felt distracted and guilty while on the clock. After conducting a time study, she discovered that her time spent working and her quality time with her daughter were actually *exactly the same*. She was spending more time with her daughter than she realized! But until she saw the raw numbers, she needlessly carried the weight of mom guilt throughout her workday.

Since our lives change and evolve over time, I recommend conducting a time study at least once a year to bring awareness to your time habits. Think of it as a routine physical or checkup on your time usage.

Time Blocking—Frequently Asked Questions

When it comes to time blocking, the rules are pretty simple: Create blocks on your calendar that represent how you will spend your time. But when you're getting started, some clarification might be helpful. Here are some questions and answers to help as you begin to take control of your time with time blocking:

- **Do you have to time block your entire day or entire week?** Not at all! In fact, it's best to leave some open or blank space to accommodate spillover and things that pop up during the week. While time blocking can combat the Planning Fallacy, even the best efforts in estimating can go awry. Ashleigh Pichon Rougelot, a high-end wedding planner and owner of Ashleigh Elizabeth Weddings & Events, uses this strategy:

  "Every day, I have three time blocks. My first two time blocks always have a specific purpose. My third time block is my 'miscellaneous' block. I don't plan anything specific during this block. Instead, I use it to finish up anything that wasn't completed in time blocks one and two, or I handle smaller one-off tasks."

- **What if I try time blocking and I get it wrong?** Keep trying. If your time blocks are consistently too long or too short, consider doing a time study to get a more accurate picture of how you're spending your time. Remember Corinn from Chapter 3 with the "meticulously underestimated" schedule that was bursting at the seams with unrealistic time blocks? After she completed her time study, she was much more honest with herself about how much time to set aside and what was possible within the boundaries of her workweek.

- **What if I don't know how long something is going to take me because I've never done it before?**
  I know exactly what this feels like. On my first day as a public relations account executive on the crisis management team at a boutique public relations firm, I was asked to create a scope and estimate for a new client, which is a planning document that establishes the scope of work for the client's project and an estimate of how many hours would be necessary to complete the work. Basically, I was being asked to estimate how long it would take me to do things I had never done before. I remember asking my supervisor, "How am I supposed to estimate how long this will take me? This is all new." Her reply? "Just make your best guess."

  When you don't know how long something will take you, you've got to give it your best guess. One way to make your guess more accurate is to break the project or task down into smaller parts. Then, think through what it might take to complete each individual part. For example, instead of trying to estimate how much time it will take you to prepare an entire report, break the report into smaller chapters or sections and estimate the time you think you'll need for each chapter.

While it's nearly impossible to accurately predict every time estimation, the more you time block, the better you'll become at time blocking.

- **How do you keep coworkers or clients from scheduling meetings over your time blocks?**
  Consider intentionally leaving space open in your week to accommodate meeting requests. For example, leave Tuesday and Thursday afternoons open for unexpected meetings. If no meetings are scheduled, you can repurpose that time for something else.

  If a coworker schedules a meeting over your time block, consider offering an alternate time. Each organization's culture and approach to meetings is going to be different. However, if you hold firm to your boundaries and politely explain that you'd designated that time for a high priority project, your coworker is more likely to understand your need to shift the meeting time.

SWISS ARMY KNIFE TOOL #2: TASK BATCHING

After my first week of mistakes as a brand-new congressional scheduler, I wised up and requested some time with a more tenured scheduler from another office. I was determined to get the hang of the job, and knew that asking an expert would fast-track me to scheduling success. This is when I was introduced to the productivity power of task batching.

A scheduler's inbox is a daily avalanche of requests and follow-ups about the status of requests. One could easily spend hours engaged in the back-and-forth of meeting maneuvers in an attempt to fit everything into the 168-hour week ahead. Instead of responding to emails from lobbyists and constituents with meeting confirmations and next steps as they landed in my inbox, I was taught to instead scan emails for the date of the request, and then organize them into folders based on the week of the request. Then, each Friday morning, I'd simply open up the folder for the upcoming week, print every email, and compile them into a binder for our chief of staff's review.

This new strategy of holding all requests until Friday morning was an absolute game changer for my week. It was so simple, yet incredibly effective. Not only did it make my life as a scheduler easier, it created a predictable routine for my chief of staff and the rest of the team who relied on the congressman's schedule to plan their week.

A few years later, thousands of miles from Capitol Hill, I employed a similar strategy while working on a campaign to elect a new secretary of state for Louisiana. Because I had the neatest handwriting on the team, I was awarded the responsibility of penning handwritten thank you notes to campaign donors. In the beginning, I'd pull out the stationery and stamps whenever I received a notification that a donation had been made.

As the campaign heated up, my list of responsibilities grew and grew. On a scrappy campaign, everyone does a little bit of everything, regardless of their title. Suddenly, I didn't have time to drop everything and write those handwritten notes. So, I started holding thank you notes until Friday afternoon. At the end of the week, I'd open up the donation spreadsheet, pull out my box of envelopes and note cards, and pour a glass of wine. By writing a week's worth of thank you notes in a batch, one after the other, I got through them quickly. Much more quickly than if I'd sprinkled them throughout the week. Waiting turned out to be a huge win.

What Is Task Batching?

Task batching, sometimes called time batching, is grouping similar tasks together and completing them all at once, one after the other.

Think about the way we do laundry. We don't wear a shirt, put that shirt in the washing machine, move that shirt to the dryer, fold the shirt, put that shirt away in a drawer, and then get another shirt to repeat the process. That would be ridiculous—and a huge waste of water, detergent, energy, and time. Instead, we toss our dirty clothes in a laundry basket; once it's full, we wash and dry a load and then fold and put away all the clothes at once. This just makes sense!

When you apply the laundry method to other parts of your life and work by task batching, you can make the most of your time, energy, and attention.

Although it might feel productive in the moment to knock out a single small task, grouping similar tasks together helps you stay focused and avoid context switching. When you group similar tasks together, you're able to stay in a consistent mindset for an extended period of time. The repetition gets you into a groove almost to the point of being able to put yourself on autopilot, especially if the batched tasks are more low-impact, menial activities.

Task batching also streamlines your workflows and increases your efficiency. The repetition enables you to notice opportunities for process improvement that you might not otherwise see when doing the same task on its own. For example, after stuffing eight envelopes, you may realize that if you position the envelope with the flap facing up, you can stuff and seal them faster. If you're task batching something like grant research for a client, you may find that creating a collection of bookmarks to relevant websites in your browser toolbar speeds up future searches.

How to Start Task Batching

Here's how to start task batching in four simple steps:

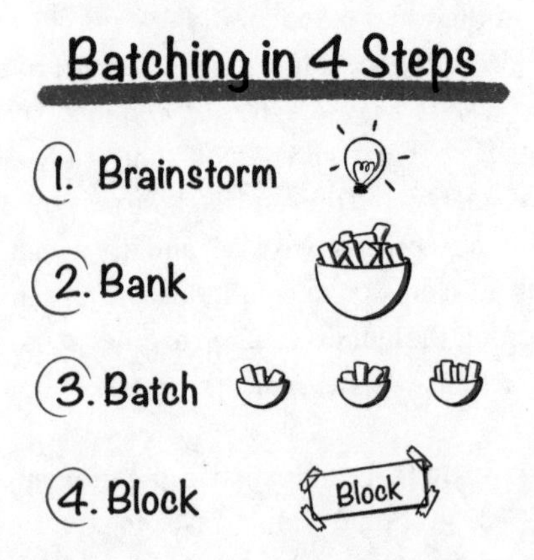

Step 1: Brainstorm

Start by brainstorming tasks you can batch. If you've conducted a time study recently, take note of the one-off tasks you performed throughout the week that could be grouped together. Did you find that you frequently checked your bank balances at random times during the week? Did you send invoices on Tuesday morning, Wednesday afternoon, and Friday night? Are you responding to emails and messages as they hit your inbox?

If you don't have time study entries to review, make a to-do list or review your existing list. This is a great starting point for identifying what tasks you can batch together. Consider zooming out from your immediate to-do list and think through the week or month as a whole. Getting a bird's-eye view of the month can help you identify those low-impact, one-off tasks that pop up throughout the month that can be batched on a recurring basis.

Be aware that many one-off tasks we perform during the week that are ideal for batching are often so small they don't make it on our official to-do lists. These are the activities that we tell ourselves, "Oh, let me just do this one thing real quick," that can kill our concentration with context switching. Capture those small tasks we often leave off to-do lists with step 2.

Step 2: Bank

Just like tossing dirty laundry in a basket, it's helpful to have a place to capture your one-off tasks that could be good candidates for batching. That's why step 2 is bank. Where will you collect your tasks until it's time to batch them? Spreadsheets, Google Docs, a project management system, or a handwritten list can serve as your "laundry basket" for task batches. As you move through your week, anytime you catch yourself doing or being tempted to do a one-off task, add that task to a list.

Step 3: Batch

Now that you've brainstormed tasks and assembled a bank of one-off tasks, it's time to start batching similar tasks together. Look at your brainstormed list and bank, and group similar items together even if those activities aren't precisely the same.

You may find that you're regularly checking account balances, sending invoices, following up with clients about the status of unpaid invoices, and reviewing your income and expenses. While each of those tasks is different, they fit nicely into a "finance batch." Drafting social media content, creating graphics, scheduling content into social media platforms, and engaging with influencers would make a fantastic "social media batch." If you currently submit travel reimbursements at random, create a "reimbursement batch." If you record interviews for your podcast, schedule your interviews into a "recording batch." If you send birthday cards or handwritten notes to clients, batch those once a month or once a week. Any small task you do multiple times during the week or month is a candidate for batching, so get creative!

A few more task batching examples to consider:

- Communication batch: respond to emails, Slack messages, and texts
- Content creation batch: draft a month's worth of blog posts, podcast episodes, or YouTube video scripts
- Recording/filming batch: record a month's worth of podcast episodes, social media short-form videos, or YouTube videos in one afternoon
- Accountability batch: send emails or text messages to check in with accountability partners and give encouragement
- Weekend planning batch: buy movie or concert tickets, make dinner reservations, schedule childcare, or make other weekend plans

Once you've set your batches, create a workflow or checklist for each one. This checklist captures the order in which you'll perform each task within the batch.

When you write down the order you'll handle the tasks within each batch, you save time that might otherwise be wasted on remembering which step comes next. Plus, when you have a checklist to reference, you're less likely to skip an important step.

Capturing your workflows also sets you up for success with delegating whether you're growing your team or moving into another role. Before I left Capitol Hill to move back to Louisiana, I handed off the scheduling binder and detailed workflow I created to the new scheduler. The transition was smooth because my processes were clearly outlined, and the new scheduler was grateful to have a proven guide to get the job done.

Step 4: Block

Once you identify your task batches, use time blocking to decide when you'll tackle each batch. Whether your batches are daily, weekly, monthly, or a different cadence altogether, making space for them on your calendar with a time block will help you remember to tackle your batches and create a more realistic schedule along the way.

When you time block your task batches, you're combating Parkinson's Law by giving your batch a set start and end time. You're combating the Planning Fallacy by estimating how much time you think you need to complete your batch, and then adding a bit more time just in case. Together, task batching and time blocking are a winning combination.

Task Batching Stumbling Blocks

While task batching is pretty straightforward, there are a few stumbling blocks that can get in the way of success. Here are a few obstacles you might encounter as you begin to implement batching:

- **What if urgent things pop up during the week that can't wait until my designated batching time block?**
  Remember the Eisenhower Matrix? If the task is truly urgent *and* important, do it now. However, sometimes things are not as urgent as they first appear. If you can, experiment with waiting until your designated batch and see what happens. If it absolutely can't wait, this particular task may not be a good fit for batching. Typically, the most ideal candidates for task batching are activities that are not urgent. It's OK and even expected that your batches will evolve over time.

- **What if some weeks my batch is big, and some weeks it's small? How can I accurately create time blocks from week to week when the size of the batch keeps changing?**
  If a task batch varies in size from week to week, consider keeping a consistent time block and using the leftover time for another low-impact task. Alternatively, consider spacing out your batches. Perhaps you only need to batch that task every other week instead of every week now that you've become more efficient.

  It also helps to keep in mind that your time blocking and task batching strategies (as well as your personal time management in general), will change and evolve over time. Experiment with different combinations of time blocking and task batching to create a schedule that works for you in that specific season of your career and life.

SWISS ARMY KNIFE TOOL #3: THEME DAYS

For many parents, the bane of their existence is school spirit week. If you're not familiar with the concept, school spirit weeks typically involve students dressing up for a different theme each day of the week. Monday might be "Crazy Hair Day." Tuesday could be "Pajama Day." On Wednesday, wear camouflage or crazy socks or dress like a pirate, and so on. While dressing up for spirit week is fun for students, it's typically the parents who scramble to find whatever the kids need to be on-theme each day.

While school theme days can be stressful, using theme days for time management is *much* more productive, and can even be fun.

What Are Theme Days?

Theme days are created by grouping similar, often repeated tasks together on a specific day of the week. It's giving each day of the week its own job or purpose.

Like task batching, theme days keep you focused on similar types of work and reduce context switching. For example, if you designate Mondays to be Marketing Monday, you spend the day in a marketing mindset. You may work on a number of different marketing tasks throughout the day, such as copywriting, content planning, or graphic design, but your overall focus is on marketing.

Assigning a theme to each weekday also means you know exactly which day you'll work on certain projects. This makes planning, decision-making, and setting expectations for yourself and others much easier.

Several years ago, as a communications manager at a museum, I implemented Social Media Mondays and Website Wednesdays. Every Monday, I created and scheduled upcoming social media content. This involved everything from gathering photos of new artwork, taking behind-the-scenes video of installations, and designing promotional graphics, to writing captions and uploading posts to our automated scheduling tool. Every Wednesday, I updated our website with new blog posts about featured artists and published details about upcoming concerts, fundraisers, and events. Plus, I made any updates requested by other departments, like adding new curators to the staff page or updating membership benefits.

Because our organization's social media and website content flowed to me from multiple departments, Social Media Monday and Website Wednesday enabled me to set expectations and deadlines with the rest of the team. Any social media requests had to be submitted by Monday morning, and website updates had to be submitted by the end of the day on Tuesday. This created a smooth rhythm of communication across the organization and encouraged my colleagues to contribute their information in a timely manner.

How to Use Theme Days to Plan Your Week

To get started with theme days, group your responsibilities into categories or buckets. You could use your task batches as a great starting point for brainstorming potential theme days. Then, once you've created your categories, decide which day of the week you'll consistently focus on those tasks. I'm a fan of using alliteration to make theme days memorable—like Marketing Monday and Finance Friday, but it's definitely not required for success.

Currently in my time management coaching business, I use these theme days to organize my week: Marketing Monday; Client Work Tuesdays, Wednesdays, and Thursdays; and Finance Fridays.

A friend at a sports marketing agency uses Tell 'Em Tuesday as a reminder to share recent client wins by submitting press releases to news outlets. This creates a consistent flow of good news for her clients, and helps her establish solid relationships with sports journalists.

A top-producing Realtor in my area designates Wednesday as Reach Out Wednesday. She writes handwritten notes to past clients, sends emails to colleagues to check in or share valuable information, and schedules coffee dates with prospective clients. She credits her success to the relationships she's intentionally cultivated over time thanks to her Reach Out Wednesdays.

If you're someone who serves a number of different clients, you could assign each client a day of the week in which you focus specifically on their projects. This creates a predictable rhythm for you and enables you to make progress with each client account instead of spending too much time on a single client while inadvertently neglecting the rest.

If your clients are in a number of different industries, you could give each industry its own day of the week. For example, you could assign Tuesdays to your tourism/hospitality clients, Wednesdays to your financial industry clients, and Thursdays to your healthcare clients.

Content creators, like podcasters, bloggers, YouTubers, social media influencers, and marketing professionals, can create a theme day for each part of the creative process. That could look like Brainstorming Monday, First Draft Tuesday, Filming Wednesday, Editing Thursday, and Publishing Friday. One of my clients, Ashley, a multichannel content creator focusing on women's fashion and beauty, utilizes Planning Tuesdays, Production Wednesdays, and Publishing Thursdays to maintain a sustainable, consistent content calendar.

You can also use a combination of both client focus and responsibility categories to create your theme days. Here's an example schedule:

- Marketing Monday
- Tourism Client Tuesday
- Financial Industry Client Wednesday
- Healthcare Client Thursday
- Finance & Administration Friday

You can base your theme days on existing standing meetings. One of my former time management clients had a standing meeting with a client every Tuesday afternoon during which she would report on potential grant opportunities. Because of this standing meeting, she designated Tuesday as Grant Research Day, and her Top 3 for the day always included a time block for researching her grant opportunities.

How to Use Theme Days at Home

Theme days aren't limited to your workday. At home, you can use theme days to create rhythms to your home maintenance activities and even your laundry! No one I know enjoys spending days buried under mountains of laundry from the past week. At our house, we use theme days to break our laundry into smaller, more manageable batches throughout the week. Our laundry theme days look like this:

- Monday: kids laundry
- Tuesday: adults laundry
- Wednesday: towels
- Thursday: bath mats
- Saturday or Sunday: sheets and towels

Theme days can also be an excellent way to simplify meal planning. A past time management coaching client, Kimberly, is a CPA, family travel blogger, and mom of four. To streamline her family's meals and weekly grocery list, she implemented theme days for dinnertime:

- Monday: Mexican
- Tuesday: chicken
- Wednesday: soup and sandwiches
- Thursday: Italian
- Friday: pizza

Giving each day its own theme made meal planning more efficient by narrowing the pool of recipes to choose from. Plus, she created variety throughout the week, and her family knew what to expect each day.

Common Questions About Theme Days

Like any time management strategy, theme days can evolve and be adapted over time. Here are some common questions about theme days:

- **Do I have to spend the entire day doing *only* things relating to my chosen theme?**
  No! You can designate a half day or whatever time frame is best for you. If something urgent and important pops up, do that regardless of your assigned theme day.

- **What if I need to take the day off? What happens to the activities on that theme day?**
  Whether it's planned or unexpected, when you have to miss a theme day use the Eisenhower Matrix to prioritize which time blocks and task batches can be pushed to the next week, and what can be rearranged to fit in the current week in order to tackle your most important work and meet deadlines. You may need to whittle off a few tasks scheduled for other days of the week in order to account for a missed day.

• • •

When you use time blocks, task batches, and theme days to plan your week, you can transform your time from being disconnected and chaotic to creating a realistic rhythm that achieves *your* version of work-life balance. When your Vision for the future is clear, and you know your Values, establish your priorities, and are aware of productivity pitfalls, this collection of basic tools is exactly what you need to make consistent progress toward your dreams.

ESSENTIAL TAKEAWAYS

- Time blocking is creating blocks on a calendar to visually represent the tasks you'll complete during that time. Time blocking combats Parkinson's Law, the Planning Fallacy, and context switching.
- Conduct a time study to get an accurate picture of how you're spending your time. Record your activities in 15- to 30-minute increments for a week, then review your time study to observe your time-use patterns.
- Task batching is grouping similar tasks together and performing them at one time. Task batching is most successful when you create a step-by-step workflow and follow the same process every time. This increases your efficiency and sets you up for delegation success.
- Create theme days by grouping similar tasks together on a specific day of the week. It's giving each day of the week its own job or purpose. Like task batching, theme days keep you focused on similar types of work and reduce context switching.

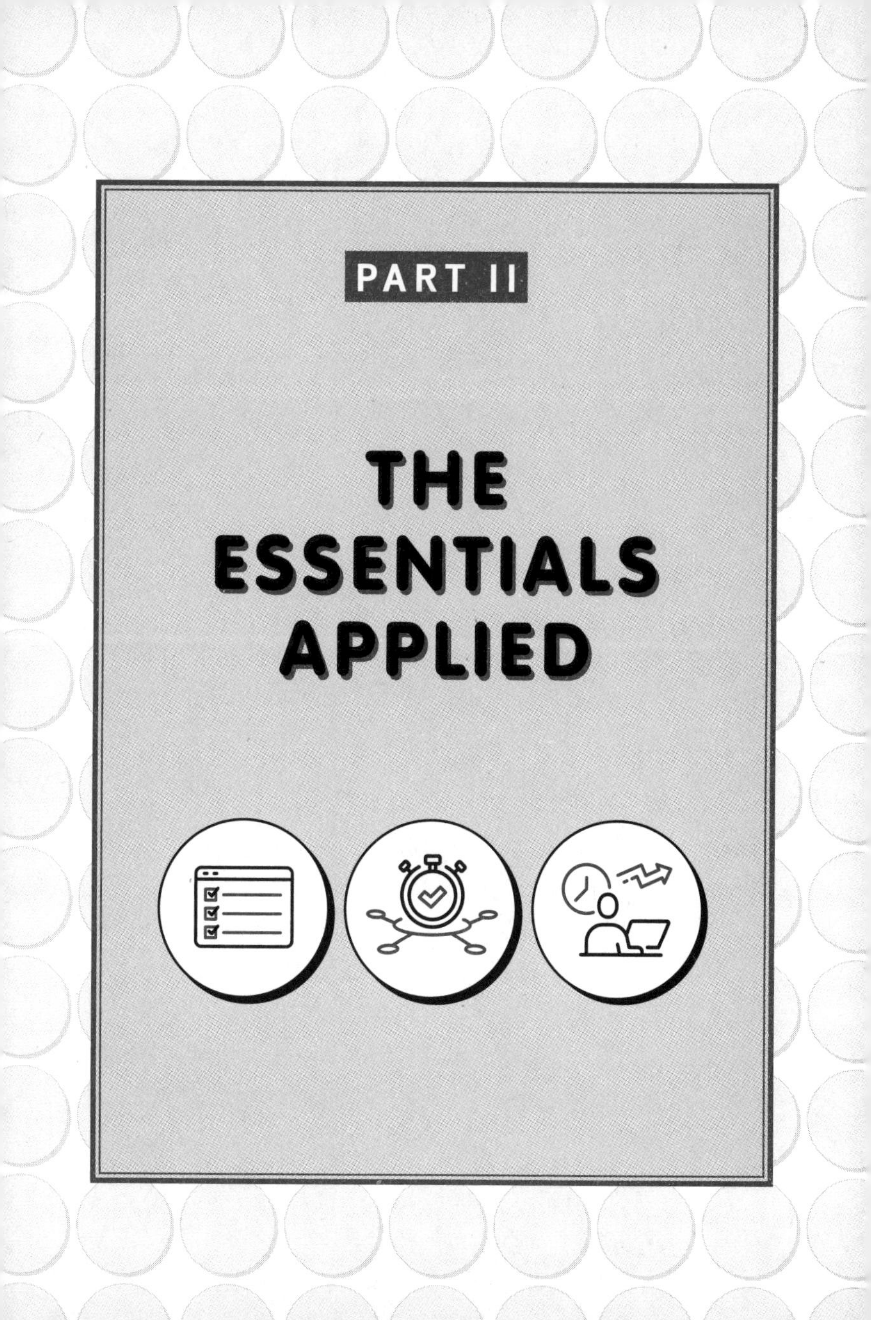
PART II
THE ESSENTIALS APPLIED

Time Management Self-Assessment

Now that you understand the essentials, you're ready to *apply* the essentials. To get started, complete the benchmark assessment below. Your answers will help highlight the areas you can target in Part II to make the most impactful improvement in your time management skills. No one else needs to see this, so feel free to be brutally honest.

Directions: Please read each statement and use the following scale to indicate how strongly you agree with it. Then add up the rating column for a total score at the bottom.

1 = Never
2 = Rarely
3 = Sometimes
4 = Usually
5 = Always

Rating	
	I have a clear Vision for what I want my future to look like.
	I have taken the time to articulate my Vision for the future.
	I understand the importance of Values and have articulated my personal Values.
	I know how to use my Vision and Values to guide decisions about how I spend my time.
	I know when I am living in alignment with my Vision and Values.

	I can clearly articulate my big-picture priorities.
	I can easily prioritize the items on my to-do list.
	Identifying my priorities for the week or day ahead comes easily to me.
	I rarely get distracted by low-impact tasks.
	I decide in advance how I will spend my time in the week ahead.
	My schedule is intentionally designed to support my Vision and Values.
	I can easily adapt my schedule when I encounter obstacles.
	Deciding how to spend my time in the week ahead comes easily to me.
	I am aware of when I am procrastinating.
	I use time blocking to plan my week.
	I use task batching to be more efficient with low-impact tasks.
	I rarely experience decision fatigue.
	I begin each week feeling calm and prepared because I have a plan.
	When I plan my week, I devise solutions for potential obstacles.
	I feel confident that my time management is moving me closer to making my Vision for the future a reality.
	Maximum Score: 100

Add up your total score to determine your percentage of the 100 possible points. This score is only the "starting line"—a way to help measure your progress as you learn more about time management in this Part, "The Essentials Applied." Once you've had a chance to practice new time management strategies, you can repeat this assessment to track your growth.

Right now, this benchmark assessment can also help you gain some valuable insights into your specific time management skill levels. Any statements that you ranked as a 4 or 5 may represent your strengths. Statements that you ranked as a 1, 2, or 3 provide you with opportunities for improvement.

Circle or highlight the three to five statements with the lowest scores. As you work through Part II and begin to practice some of your time management skills in real time, pay close attention to those specific areas. If you focus on accelerating those particular skills, you'll likely see the biggest change in your time management and productivity.

Block Your Boulders

Lauren was exasperated by her cluttered garage. Cluttered is actually a bit of an understatement. Her two-car garage was filled to the brim with sports gear, tools, random boxes that were never unpacked after moving in, bikes, bags, holiday decorations, and who knows what else. The mess had gotten so out of control that she and her husband were forced to park in their driveway, which was incredibly inconvenient during an unusually rainy and humid summer.

After several attempts to organize the mess herself, she finally gave up and called a professional. No matter how she tried to organize, categorize, and rearrange the stuff in the garage, there was never enough room to park the cars. When the organizer arrived early one sunny Saturday morning, they worked together to remove every single thing taking up space in the garage. Every box, bag, tool, and toy was pulled out and placed on the lawn, leaving a cavernous, empty space.

After giving the empty garage a good surface clean, Lauren was ready to begin sorting through all the stuff. Since everything that was previously in the garage was now out on display in the yard, she wanted to hurry to get it all back inside. But, the professional organizer had other plans.

"All right, go ahead and park your cars in the garage and we'll get to work," she said.

Lauren put her hands on her hips, cocked her head, and furrowed her brows, clearly confused. "Wait. I'm sorry. What? We're putting the cars in *first*? How are we going to fit everything else back in?"

The organizer replied, "What's most important here? Parking your cars in the garage, or having room for all of this stuff? Remember why we're doing this."

After Lauren reluctantly pulled both cars into the garage, they got to work. They started with the larger items first, finding space for the tool bench, bikes, and pink battery-powered Barbie Jeep. Then came the medium-sized items. The sports gear and the golf clubs were given a home. The holiday decorations were stacked together in the corner. Finally, all that was left were small, random things. Odds and ends that could be tucked out of sight into baskets and bins. Stuff that could be thrown away. Broken toys that were missing pieces. Cleaning supplies that could be relocated to other spots inside the home. Baby gear that could be stored in the attic until it was needed again. A pile of donations had even started to accumulate.

Everything that *needed* a home in the garage now had its own space, including the two most important items—their cars. Lauren was shocked. By keeping her Purpose in mind (freeing up space for their cars) and putting the two largest, highest priority items (the cars) in the garage first, every subsequent decision about what to keep and where to place it was just a little easier. They started with what mattered most, and then found space for the large, medium, and small things until everything fell into place.

When you know your Purpose using your Vision and Values as your direction and guiding principles, the practice of prioritizing becomes just a bit easier. I intentionally use the word *practice* here because like most things, your priorities will adapt and evolve with the ebbs and flows of life. Setting your priorities isn't something you do once and then move on. As you master time management, you'll find that you're in an almost constant state of prioritization to address the myriad requests, opportunities, and obstacles that come your way.

In Part I, you learned about the Pareto principle, the origin of the word *priority*, and how to use the Eisenhower Matrix to decide what to do next when *everything* feels important. In this chapter, we'll take all of that one step further by learning a method you can use to prioritize just about anything based on your unique roles and responsibilities. Plus, we'll take the sometimes abstract and confusing topic of priorities and transform it into something you can see, touch, and easily understand. So, let's get to it.

BOULDERS, BIG ROCKS, AND PEBBLES

One thing I've found when discussing the concept of priorities with friends, family, and coaching clients alike is that priorities can feel abstract and confusing. We know that a priority is something that's important. We know we're supposed to have our priorities in order. We now know that a priority was originally intended to be one thing, the *first* thing. But none of that makes stacking our things to do in order of importance any easier.

Instead of thinking of all priorities as simply "important," I like to transform the idea of priorities into something we're all familiar with. Something we can touch and feel. Something real. Something like rocks. Boulders, Big Rocks, and Pebbles, to be precise.

Just as the Pareto principle tells us that some stuff is more important than other stuff, thinking of the way you fulfill your roles and carry out your responsibilities as Boulders, Big Rocks, and Pebbles gives weight to the different tasks and to-dos in your life. If you've ever heard of the pickle jar theory, or the parable of the pickle jar, this is my variation. As I explain each type of priority, think about what in your life falls into each category. What are *your* Boulders, Big Rocks, and Pebbles?

Boulders

I've never been to the Grand Canyon, but whenever I hear the word *boulder*, I immediately picture the giant, red orange rock formations pictured in my elementary school geography textbook. I imagine what it might be like to push on one of those massive stones with all of my might, feeling absolutely no give and no movement, regardless of how much effort is put into the push. Boulders are steadfast and immovable.

Your Boulder priorities represent what matters most to you. They're the things that help you be your best self. Boulder priorities move you closer to achieving your Vision for the future. They're your Values in action.

Meditation, working out, intentionally cultivating relationships, and calling your grandmother are all potential Boulders. Time spent doing personal or professional development, reading a book about time management essentials, and spending quality time with your children could fall within the Boulder category, too. They're all activities that help you grow, or there's an element of self-care, or they keep you happy and healthy.

Your Boulders are obviously important, but what sets them apart is that they're *not urgent*. In most cases, no one is relying on you to follow through with a Boulder activity. Rarely are you on deadline to meditate for 10 minutes. The consequences of skipping a workout are felt by no one but you. Your personal or professional development? Also up to you.

Even though Boulders are clearly important, because they're not typically urgent, they can easily be put on the back burner. We tell ourselves that we'll get to them if we have time. That we'll spend quality time with our partners once we finish our project. That we'll plan that vacation once we get to a good stopping point with work. We'll finish our kids' baby books or print those photos when we have more time. Spoiler alert: The perfect time, or enough time, will never magically appear. That's why we need to make time for these important, but not urgent Values-focused activities.

Sometimes important standing team meetings or client meetings can be classified as Boulders if they truly support the work of your team. They're important, but not urgent, and the benefits of bringing your team together to reinforce your culture, strengthen your bonds, and be brought up to speed on the status of projects is what gives this type of meeting Boulder status. If a standing meeting is a good use of time and foundational for your team, it can be a professional Boulder. However, not every standing meeting meets these criteria. Some may be classified as Big Rocks and even Pebbles based on their level of urgency and importance, which we'll get to soon enough.

Our routines are also examples of Boulders, especially the five essential routines. Your morning, evening, workday startup, workday shutdown, and weekly planning routines are the milestones within your day and your week that set you up for success.

Routine 1: Morning

The way you start your day sets the tone for the rest of the day. Your morning routine takes you from asleep to awake to ready for whatever the day brings. In addition to the basics—dressing, getting your kids ready for school, and having breakfast—your morning is also an ideal time for personal development.

Many effective leaders and successful business owners carve out time in the morning for reading personal development books, spiritual devotions, meditation, prayer, affirmations, visualization, and exercise. Putting these Boulder priorities at the top of your day and making them a part of your morning routine ensures they're tackled before the unpredictability of the day sets in.

Routine 2: Evening

Your evening routine helps you wind down from a busy day and prepare for a good night's sleep. It could include preparing for the next morning, shutting off electronic devices at a specific time, completing skin care rituals, reading, and doing any habits that ease you into bedtime mode so you can get the recommended seven to nine hours of shut-eye.

Routine 3: Workday Startup

A workday startup routine is like the morning routine of your workday. It's a short series of actions repeated at the beginning of each workday to transition into a working mindset. It pairs mental boundaries with physical activities that send a signal to your brain that it's time to get down to business.

A workday startup routine is especially important if you work remotely. When you work from home, the boundaries between work and home can become very blurry and result in unclear start and end times. When you have a workday startup routine, you're able to create a mental environment for focus without even leaving your home.

A workday startup routine could include opening your laptop, reviewing the day's schedule, opening your task management system, and writing your Top 3 priorities for the day at the top of your notebook—maybe while drinking a (hopefully still hot) cup of coffee.

Routine 4: Workday Shutdown

Just like the workday startup routine, a workday shutdown routine helps you close out your workday in a structured way so you can start fresh the next morning and can be present with your family and friends once the workday is over.

A typical workday shutdown routine may include reviewing tomorrow's schedule, closing your browser tabs or windows, closing your laptop, and placing your notebook on top of your closed laptop. Many people often joke that they have too many tabs open in their brain. This routine literally closes your tabs so you (and your computer) have an opportunity to rest, recharge, and attack tomorrow refreshed and ready to go.

If the thought of closing your tabs makes your eye twitch, this doesn't have to be part of your routine! Whatever works for you is all that matters when having an effective workday shutdown routine. My friend Katie, for example, works from home at a desk in her bedroom. Every day while working, she wears a cozy cardigan. Then, at the end of her workday, she takes it off and changes into something else. This simple switch signals that her workday is done, and she transitions into a "home" mindset.

Routine 5: Weekly Planning Session

Your Weekly Planning Session routine is your opportunity to get a bird's-eye view of the week ahead, make a lot of decisions at once, and step into your week feeling calm, prepared, and ready for anything. We'll dive into the nuts and bolts of Weekly Planning Sessions in Chapter 7, but a typical Weekly Planning Session includes reviewing your calendar, creating time blocks for your most important work, mapping out any travel or commute time, identifying potential obstacles, and planning your meals for the week ahead.

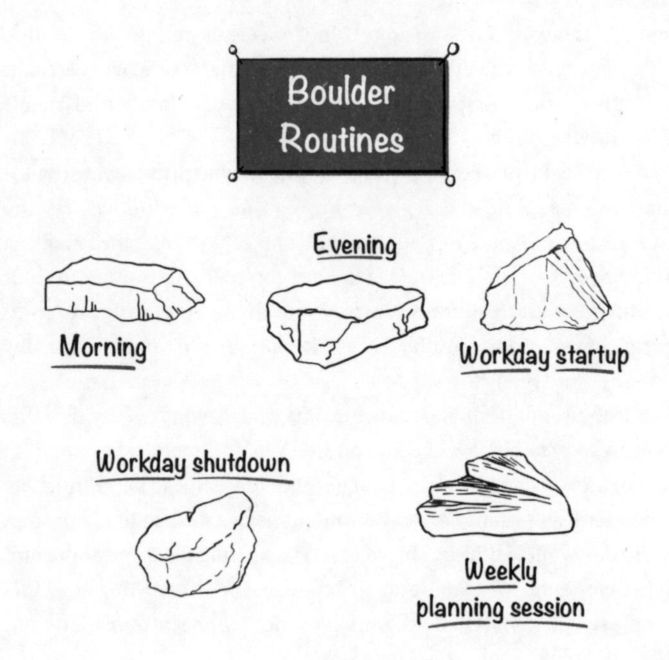

• • •

There are certainly other routines besides these essential five that qualify as Boulders. In fact, any routine that helps you feel energized, refreshed, and ready deserves Boulder status. But, if you start with these five, you'll establish a solid foundation on which to build your entire week.

Exercise: Identify Your Boulder Priorities

Now that we know Boulder priorities help you show up as the best version of yourself in your roles and responsibilities, it's time to get clear on what your Boulders are. In this exercise, you'll identify your Boulder priorities so you can be more intentional about scheduling them in your calendar.

Remember, Boulder priorities include your routines and the team meetings that help your team perform at its highest level. And, because they're usually not urgent, they can sometimes be pushed until there's "enough time." By starting to shift your mindset and think of these as immovable, you'll be less tempted to put them on the back burner.

Step 1: Open your calendar and review the previous two weeks. What examples of Boulders are currently present in your schedule?

Step 2: Identify what Boulders you need to make time for that aren't represented in your schedule. For example, a regular call to check in with your grandmother may be a Boulder that is not currently on your calendar. Additionally, your routines may not be blocked in your schedule even though you do them on a regular basis. Block time for those Boulders in your calendar in order to hold space for them.

Step 3: Determine what Boulders you would like to add to your life based on your roles and responsibilities. Once you have that list, think about how you can make time for them. You may need to rearrange your existing schedule and add time blocks to represent your Boulders to ensure you have the space to spend time doing these important, but not urgent, activities that help you show up as your best self.

Big Rocks

Like Boulders, your Big Rock priorities are also important, but the biggest difference is that Big Rock priorities are *urgent*. They aren't necessarily crisis-level, on-fire urgent, but there's some type of deadline involved and sometimes they're project-based. If you think back to the Eisenhower Matrix from Part I, Big Rock priorities fall squarely into the top left quadrant. These are things you need to do now, or at least you will need to get to them soon.

In addition to being urgent, what makes Big Rock priorities important is that they're impactful, needle-moving activities. It's strategizing a new project at work, writing a chapter of your book, working on your dissertation, interviewing a candidate for an important role that needs to be filled on your team, preparing a proposal for a potential client, or anything that moves you closer to reaching a goal that helps make your Purpose a reality.

While we tend to think of Big Rocks in a professional sense, they're also very present in your personal life. Big Rocks in your personal life could look like planning a fundraiser for a nonprofit organization where you volunteer. Renovating your guest bathroom, planning your daughter's first birthday party, and hosting a yard sale are all examples of personal Big Rocks.

The Big Difference Between Boulders and Big Rocks

You might be wondering, if Big Rocks are both important *and* urgent, why aren't they Boulders? Boulders are bigger than Big Rocks, and these Big Rocks sound pretty darn important since they're also urgent. Here's why: Usually there's some flexibility involved with your Big Rocks. If you push a Big Rock, it's not completely immovable like a Boulder. Yes, even though some Big Rocks are more urgent than others, in most cases there's some wiggle room with timing. That wiggle room is what enables us to create realistic project timelines, whether that project is personal or professional—and what makes them Big Rocks (not Boulders).

Another important difference between Big Rocks and Boulders is that even though they both get you closer to making your Vision a reality, only Boulders are truly foundational to your personal health and well-being.

Boulders enable you to excel at your Big Rocks. Having a solid morning routine (Boulder) enables you to bring your best self to leading an important meeting at work (Big Rock). Having a predictable workday shutdown routine (Boulder) enables you to be present as you give your time to other endeavors like volunteer work or home projects (Big Rocks) in the evening. Making time for fitness and caring for your mental health (both Boulders) keep you healthy so you can give your best focus to your most important, needle-moving projects (Big Rocks).

Exercise: Name Your Big Rock Priorities

With these big differences between Boulders and Big Rocks in mind, here are your next steps:

Step 1: Review your schedule from the previous two weeks. What examples of Big Rocks are currently present in your life?

Step 2: Ask yourself: How do my Boulders support my Big Rocks? Are there any Boulders I should consider adding to support my Big Rocks?

Step 3: Identify what Big Rocks you would like to add to your life based on your roles and responsibilities. How can you arrange your schedule to make time for them?

Pebbles

Simply put, Pebble priorities include everything that's *not* a Boulder or a Big Rock. They're little things that take up space on our to-do lists that aren't important or urgent. Pebble priorities don't contribute to your health and well-being, like Boulders. Unlike Big Rocks, they don't have a huge impact on your projects or the activities that move you closer to your Vision.

Instead, Pebbles are mostly maintenance tasks and include things like making a dentist's appointment, signing a field trip permission slip, rescheduling a meeting, sending a birthday card, or submitting a reimbursement request to the finance department. These things need to be done, but they don't necessarily have a highly important time stamp.

Pebbles are actually easy to tackle, but the problem is they can steal all of our productive time if we don't watch out for them. If you've ever reached the end of your day and felt exhausted because you were busy all day long, but you didn't actually accomplish anything important, you got lost in the Pebbles. Pebbles are busywork, and even though you might *feel* productive jumping around from Pebble to Pebble, you're not making any progress. That hamster-wheel of running but going nowhere feeling? Pebbles are to blame.

Another problem with Pebbles is that we typically have a lot of them to deal with. Pebbles and the Pareto principle can show up on your to-do list as well. On any given day, your to-do list is likely 80 percent Pebbles and 20 percent Boulders and Big Rocks. Remember, in many cases, 20 percent of the inputs produce 80 percent of the outputs. That means that only around 20 percent of your to-do list is going to be truly impactful. Fortunately, I have four strategies that you can use to keep your Pebbles under control.

Pebble Strategy 1: Categorize Your To-Do List

Next time you make your to-do list for the day, take a moment to note each type of priority present on your list. If something is a Boulder, put a "B" next to that item. If it's a Big Rock, put a "BR." If it's a Pebble, put a small "p" next to it. This practice of categorizing your tasks based on priority will hone your prioritization skills. With each of your tasks and to-dos labeled, you'll be more likely to focus on the Boulders and Big Rocks that will move you closer to your Vision.

Pebble Strategy 2: Push the Pebbles Down

As you become more and more proficient with prioritizing your tasks, keep your Pebbles separate from your Boulders and Big Rocks. One simple method for separating your tasks on a daily to-do list is to write Boulders and Big Rocks starting on the top line of the page and working your way down. Then, start your Pebbles on the last line of the page and work your way up. This creates a visual separation between your most important tasks and your busywork, and it reinforces that Pebbles are less important because they're lower on the page. If you have a few spare minutes and you can't tackle your next Boulder or Big Rock, scan your Pebbles and choose a few to cross off your list.

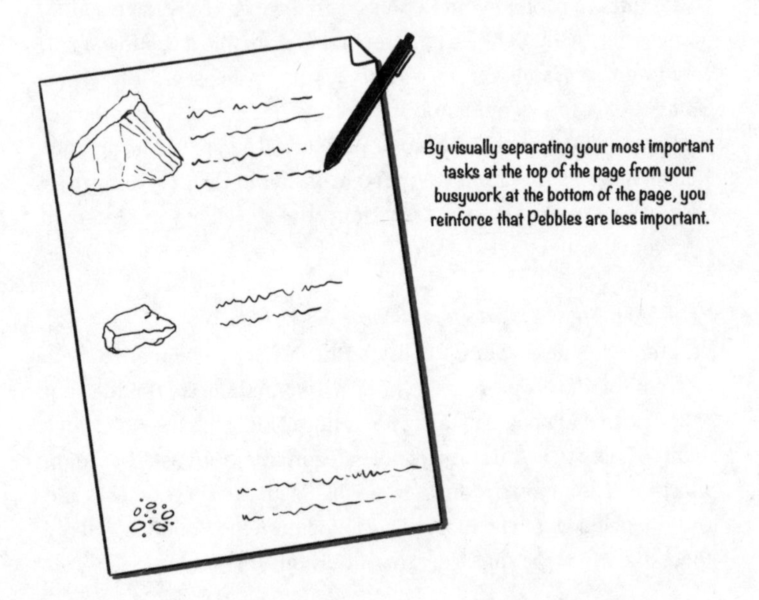

By visually separating your most important tasks at the top of the page from your busywork at the bottom of the page, you reinforce that Pebbles are less important.

Pebble Strategy 3: Transform the Pebbles into Big Rocks

Yes, it's possible to squeeze together a bunch of Pebbles and create a new Big Rock. The secret? Task batching. When you create a batch of similar Pebbles, you can maximize the time you spend and create a bigger impact. On its own, writing a single thank you note to a fundraising donor might be deemed a Pebble. However, writing 25 thank you notes in a single time block could qualify as a Big Rock because of the size of the impact and the relevance to the overarching fund-raising goal. Similarly, sending a single invoice could be considered a Pebble. But checking the balances of all of your accounts, transferring funds, paying bills, sending invoices, following up with clients regarding unpaid invoices, categorizing expenses, and reviewing financial statements in one workflow definitely qualifies as a financially focused Big Rock.

Pebble Strategy 4: Schedule a Pebble Power Hour

Another way to create a Big Rock out of your Pebbles is to collect all of your unrelated Pebbles in one place. Typically, a task batch is made up of similar tasks that are done together, but sometimes there are those random, nonurgent tasks that aren't similar to anything, but still need to get done. Changing a burned out light bulb in the ceiling fan and updating an address in your Christmas card list aren't related, but if they don't fit in another category, you can group them and tackle them both at once.

Add these one-off Pebbles to a separate list or a specific place in your task management system. Then, add a Pebble Power Hour to your schedule. During Pebble Power Hour, knock out as many random Pebbles as you can, one after the other. Having a recurring weekly, monthly, or bimonthly Pebble Power Hour gives these random tasks a home in your schedule and removes the temptation to waste productive focus time on low-impact tasks.

PRIORITIES ROCK

Remember Lauren's cars that couldn't fit in the garage? They were Boulders that were being put on the back burner until she had more space. But that space was impossible to find because of all of the Big Rocks and Pebbles that had taken over the garage. Once she, with the help of her organizer, got clear on what mattered most and put the Boulders in first, the Big Rocks and Pebbles were whittled down until they fit into place. Your projects, tasks, and to-dos can be approached the exact same way.

Priorities don't have to be abstract or confusing at all. In fact, priorities can totally rock. Pun intended. When you start by grounding yourself in your roles and responsibilities, using Boulders, Big Rocks, and Pebbles is a great way to make prioritizing everything in your life come easily. Your Boulders are the immovable foundation that help you show up as the best version of yourself. Your Big Rocks propel you toward your Vision for the future. Pebbles are necessary, but if you're strategic you won't let Pebbles get the best of you. In Chapter 7, we'll take our Boulders, Big Rocks, and Pebbles and strategically arrange them to design your Ideal Week with space for what matters most.

What matters most to you and helps you show up as your best self

Big Rocks

Urgent & important, high-impact activities in your life and work

Pebbles

Low-value, low-impact tasks

ESSENTIAL TAKEAWAYS

- Your Boulder priorities represent what matters most to you and help you be your best self. They're your Values in action and move you closer to achieving your Vision for the future.
- Big Rock priorities are the urgent and important activities in your life and work that move you closer to achieving your Vision. High-impact, high-value activities, they represent your most important work.
- Pebbles are the low-value, low-impact tasks that take up space on to-do lists. If we're not careful, we can easily spend too much time engaged in Pebble-driven busywork.

Design Your Ideal Week

Picture this: It's Friday afternoon. You're relaxed, and there's not an ounce of stress in sight. You're capping off the end of another great week. You got enough sleep. You crossed just about everything off your to-do list, and anything remaining can easily wait until next week. Each of your personal Values was represented on your calendar. You made time for personal development, your mornings were relatively stress-free, and you felt present and engaged with your friends and family during your downtime.

You smile as you look forward to your plans for the weekend. Babysitters are confirmed and reservations are made. Sunday scaries? Not for you. When you think about Monday, you're energized because you know exactly what your focus will be next week and how it supports your Vision for the future.

Does this sound like a dream to you? A fairy tale even? It's not. Or, it doesn't have to be. This dream life is possible, and making it your reality is simpler than you might think.

BEGIN WITH THE END IN MIND

A contractor would never start building a house without a blueprint. A civil engineer wouldn't begin constructing a bridge without a detailed plan. In both of these cases and more, a version of the finished product is created *before* the concrete is poured or the first nail is hammered.

A detailed plan serves multiple purposes in a building project. It aids in creating a timeline and in budgeting for the cost of materials and labor. A detailed plan also gets everyone involved on the same page, and it is a reference to turn to in moments of conflict or confusion. Plus, a detailed plan can serve as a guide or template for future projects that are similar, eliminating the need to start from scratch or reinvent the wheel.

One of Stephen Covey's habits in his book *The 7 Habits of Highly Effective People* is "Begin with the end in mind." For us, beginning with the end in mind is to embark on your day, on a task, or on a project, with a clear Vision of the outcome you hope to achieve. It's starting with your Purpose, instead of just starting.

We live in a society that prioritizes action. As a coach with a primarily online business, I hear online marketing gurus shouting, "Take imperfect action!" from their digital rooftops nearly every day. Just yesterday, in fact, I came across the recommendation from one thought leader to "Ready. Fire! Aim" instead of "Ready. Aim. Fire!" It was meant to be an encouragement to act first and think later, but honestly it just sounds a bit dangerous. The age-old advice to "look before you leap," and the reminder from my mother to my childhood extroverted self to "think before you speak" could use a resurgence when it comes to the way we think about our time.

When I look around, I see scores of people *doing*. Always doing. And buying into the false belief that if you're not doing *something*, you're not doing enough. That you have to be constantly moving in order to move forward. But, somewhere along the way, we've forgotten the importance and absolute necessity of thinking and planning. Instead, we just jump right in and start building our weeks like a house without a blueprint. We dive into projects without thinking through the milestones that indicate progress and what the finished product should look like. We walk into meetings without an agenda. We don't ask ourselves or our colleagues, "What does success look like for this project?" Then, we wonder why everything falls apart before we reach the finish line.

This chapter is dedicated to designing *your* most important blueprint: your Ideal Week.

WHAT IS AN IDEAL WEEK?

An Ideal Week is a template for how you'd like to spend your time each week. Similar to an artist's sketch, an architect's blueprints, or a designer's renderings, your Ideal Week is a built out, time-blocked week that contains everything you *need* to do, and everything you *want* to do. It's also something you can use over and over as a guide, instead of approaching each new week like an overwhelming blank canvas.

Imagine that you can suspend reality, clear your calendar, and plan the best week possible that includes time for work, time for your routines, time for self-care like working out or meditation, time with friends and family, and time for life maintenance like grocery shopping and managing your finances. What would that week look like? What would you do on each day? When would you work out? When would you work on specific projects? How much time would you allot for grocery shopping or self-care? That's what we're going to work on in this chapter.

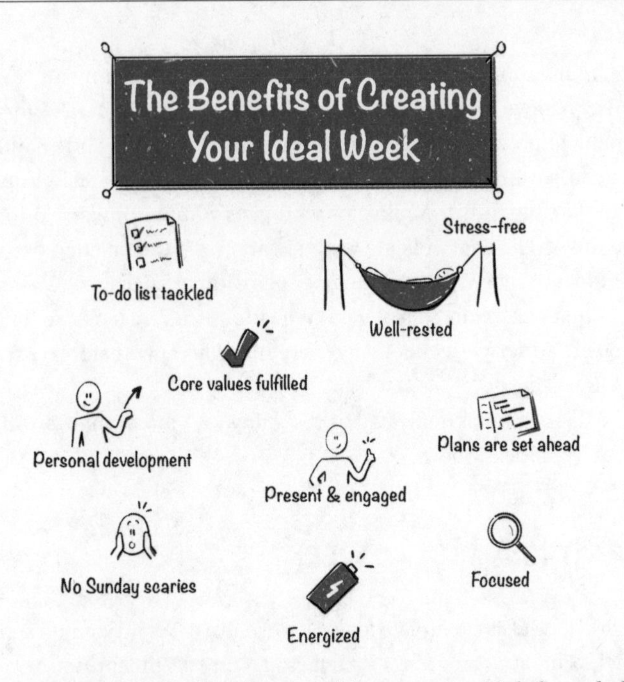

Designing an Ideal Week starts with pausing to think through the life you'd *actually* like to live from week to week, instead of jumping in and just seeing what happens. It's *designing* your week and making decisions in advance about how you'd like to spend your time. It's saying *no* to flying by the seat of your pants, and instead approaching each week with a plan.

What an Ideal Week Gives You

While there are countless benefits to designing an Ideal Week, three of the most notable impacts are reduced decision fatigue, more consistent rhythms and routines, and firmer boundaries:

- **Reduced decision fatigue**
  Decision fatigue is the feeling we have when we've made so many decisions that our decision-making abilities start to decline. Having an Ideal Week to guide how you spend your time preserves some of that decision-making power so you can save it for the decisions that really matter.

- **More consistent rhythms and routines**
  Having predictable routines improves sleep and overall health, reduces stress, improves focus, and maximizes productivity. An Ideal Week is the ultimate routine because it creates a repeatable flow you can follow week after week.

- **Firmer boundaries**
  When you have an Ideal Week, you're able to create representations of your boundaries using time blocks. When you can see your boundaries, a new layer of accountability is created and you're more likely to stick to them.

THE BIG DIFFERENCE BETWEEN IDEAL AND PERFECT

Before diving into actually designing your Ideal Week, I want to address perfection. When designing your Ideal Week, we're not creating a perfect, flawless week. It's called an "Ideal" Week for a reason.

First of all, there's no such thing as perfect. Your Ideal Week is not a measuring stick of how good you are at time management. Nor is it meant to create pressure that you must stick to every single minute of your plan for the week. Aiming for absolute perfection in your schedule is a fast track to disappointment and frustration. Life happens.

Curveballs happen. Plans change. We have to adapt our plans to meet those curveballs.

So, what exactly is the difference between perfect and ideal? *Perfect* means without fault, or flawless. *Ideal*, on the other hand, means the optimal, or best, possibility.

Your Ideal Week is a map of the ideal possibility for your week, with the understanding that it will not be executed flawlessly. Your Ideal Week on paper may never actually happen in reality.

If you're scratching your head and wondering *why* we're spending time designing an Ideal Week that may never even exist in the real world, I've got you covered. Even though your carefully crafted Ideal Week may never be perfectly executed down to the minute, just like defining your Values, the power is in the *process*.

The process of thinking through and visualizing what your Ideal Week might look like will cause you to make purposeful decisions about how you spend your time. It's like creating a mood board or a Pinterest board for a design project. Sorting through all the different decor styles, furniture types, and color schemes helps you narrow down what you like, and what you don't. Just like a mood board helps you refine your style, creating an Ideal Week inspired by your Vision, Values, and priorities helps you further refine what matters most.

HOW TO DESIGN YOUR IDEAL WEEK

Congratulations! You've already done most of the work that goes into designing your Ideal Week! How? Because you've created your Vision for the future; defined your Values; thought through your roles and responsibilities; and identified your Boulders, Big Rocks, and Pebbles. All of that work means you're already halfway there! Before we get started and put pen to paper, grab your Vision, Values, and priorities notes so you can refer back to them as you think through your week.

Step 1: Choose Your Calendar

To design your Ideal Week, we'll begin by suspending reality and starting with a blank slate. Your first step is to decide where that blank slate will live. You have three options to choose from—a digital calendar, paper planner, or printed calendar pages.

Digital Calendar

I recommend creating a new blank calendar in your digital calendar of choice. While I can't provide the step-by-step instructions for creating a blank digital calendar in every calendar platform, both Google Calendar and Outlook allow you to create new calendars that can be toggled on and off. Create your new calendar and title it "Ideal Week."

If you currently use a paper planner to manage your time, I encourage you to test-drive Google Calendar specifically. Creating a Google account is completely free, and the time you save by creating time blocks that you can drag and drop, color-code, and customize is well worth learning a new tool. Plus, you can access and update your calendar from your smartphone using an app, and you don't have to worry about messy scratch outs, scribbles, or correction fluid when you need to make changes.

Paper Planner with a Vertical Weekly Layout

If you're not interested in a digital calendar, find an unused weekly spread in your paper planner. Ideally, this spread should include the full week, Sunday through Saturday, and have a vertical grid layout that denotes the hours in each day from at least 6 a.m. to 9 p.m. Anything less won't include enough hours to design your Ideal Week, and a weekly layout that only features open boxes for each day won't provide the structure needed to design your week.

	SUNDAY	MONDAY	TUESDAY	WEDNESDAY	THURSDAY	FRIDAY	SATURDAY
6 a.m.							
7 a.m.							
8 a.m.							
9 a.m.							
10 a.m.							
11 a.m.							
12 p.m.							
1 p.m.							
2 p.m.							
3 p.m.							
4 p.m.							
5 p.m.							
6 p.m.							
7 p.m.							
8 p.m.							
9 p.m.							

Printed Calendar Pages

Finally, if your paper planner doesn't include a vertical weekly layout, find a printable blank weekly planning sheet online. Head to annadkornick.com/essentials to download a free printable weekly planning sheet created for this exact purpose. Consider printing a few copies so you can create several iterations and then finalize your completed Ideal Week. I've personally had success with this method in the past using trimmed sticky notes to create one-hour and 30-minute time blocks that I could easily reposition as well as different colored highlighters and pens to visually organize the week.

Step 2: Block Your Boulders

Remember Lauren and her car conundrum from the previous chapter? She and her husband couldn't fit their cars in the garage because it was overflowing with everything *except* their cars. After she completely emptied the space to create a blank slate, her next step was to park the cars where they belonged, in the garage. Parking the cars *first* enabled Lauren to place everything else back in the garage *around* the cars.

That's exactly what we're going to do with our Boulder priorities. Remember, Boulders are important, but not urgent and can easily be placed on the back burner in favor of handling more urgent Big Rocks or easy but low-impact Pebbles. To protect our Boulders, we're going to put them in our Ideal Week *first*, and allow everything else to fit around them. What are your Boulders? Go ahead and pull those from your list and add them in accordingly.

Here are a few Boulders to consider blocking in your Ideal Week first:

- Seven to nine hours of sleep
- Some physical activity a few times a week
- An actual lunch break
- Activities that represent your Values and help you show up as your best self in your roles and responsibilities

For each Boulder, estimate approximately how much time you need or want to spend on each activity. Then, create a time block of that length and place it on your calendar. As you're creating your time blocks, remember that we consistently underestimate how long things

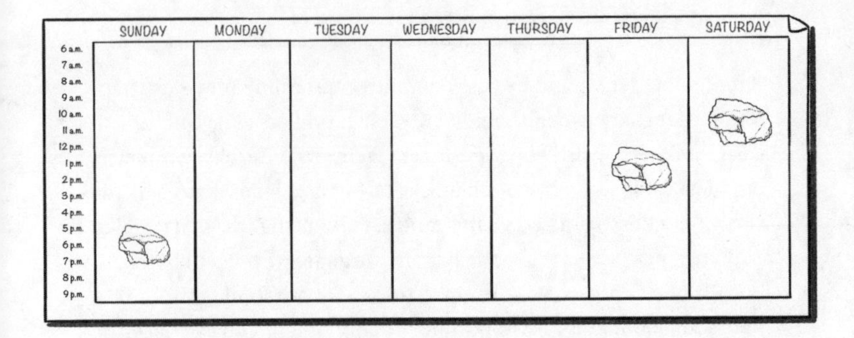

take us, so consider adding some extra time just to be safe. If you're using color-coding to visually organize your Ideal Week, consider making all your Boulders the same color so they stand out as being the most important, steadfast things you do each week.

One interesting Boulder concept to consider is a No Meeting Day. Many companies like Clockwise, Atlassian, and Shopify have implemented companywide No Meeting Days to protect their employees' focus time. A No Meeting Day is exactly like it sounds: one day per week is completely off-limits to meetings. This increases your available time for focus and creates space for you to work on your most important projects. The most successful No Meeting Days are consistent from week to week because they establish a rhythm and set expectations with others. If you're considering implementing a No Meeting Day, include it in your Ideal Week.

Step 3: Add Standing Meetings

Once you've blocked your personal and professional Boulders, add in your existing standing meetings. In this step, we begin to see the

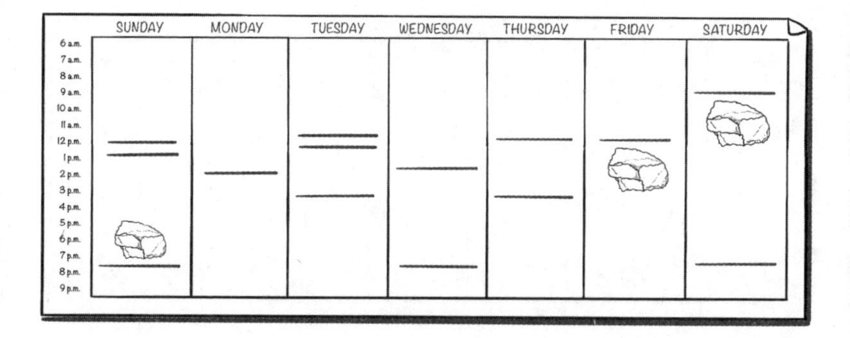

reality of our Ideal Weeks. Often, valuable standing meetings, such as recurring client meetings, team syncs, all-hands staff meetings, and department meetings are examples of professional Boulders. They support your most important work and help the team work better together.

In most cases, we don't have too much control over the time and cadence of our standing meetings. However, if you *do* have control, examine these meetings critically to determine whether they should stay in place as scheduled, be moved to a more opportune time, decrease in frequency, or be shortened to optimize your schedule. Additionally, if you're a leader and you *don't* have regular, recurring meetings with your team, consider this an opportunity to end random meeting times and establish a consistent meeting rhythm.

Step 4: Create Space for Your Routines

Next, it's time to create time blocks for each of the five essential routines: morning, evening, workday startup, workday shutdown, and Weekly Planning Session.

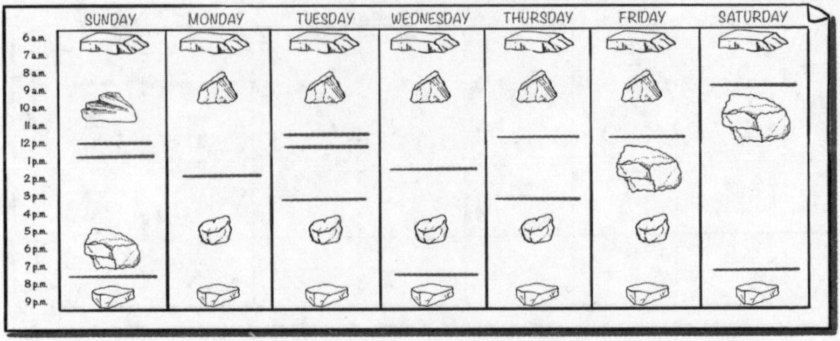

To create an accurate time block for your routines, write out each step of your routine, estimate how long each step will take you, and use that information to determine your ideal start and end time. You may find that you'll need to cut certain pieces of your routines, or move those pieces to other parts of your day. For example, if your ideal morning routine necessitates waking up at 4 a.m. to get through every step, see what you can move to your evening routine. Perhaps instead of preparing your kids' lunches in the morning, you can move lunch prep to your evening routine or batch prepping on Sunday evenings.

Step 5: Assess Your Open Space

Now that you've blocked your Boulders, added your standing meetings, and created space for your routines, it's time to assess your open space. Since our goal is to be consistent from week to week with our Boulders, this open space represents the amount of time you have each week for variation. Typically, this is when my time management coaching clients or Ideal Week workshop participants experience one of two light bulb moments. Either they realize that they have way more available time than they originally thought, *or* they're faced with the reality that they actually have *less* time than they imagined.

When you finally have a complete visual of what your week looks like with all of the essentials added, you begin to see that the 37-point to-do lists you've been creating are completely unrealistic. No wonder you've never made it to the end of your list! There just aren't enough hours in the day to tackle the unrealistic load you've been placing on yourself.

Regardless of which light bulb moment you have, I hope it's soon followed by a feeling of relief. With a realistic view of your week, you can now create a realistic to-do list. One that enables you to end your days and weeks feeling accomplished, because instead of filling your list of tasks to the brim, you're able to "right size" your list and make it achievable.

Your open space is where we'll place your Big Rocks and Pebbles. Like Lauren's garage, we're going to put things *around* the Boulders. And that might involve cutting some things in the process.

Step 6: Drop in Your Big Rocks

Now that your Boulders are in place, it's time to add your Big Rocks. Remember, Big Rocks are the important, urgent tasks that move the needle in your life and work. They're usually project-based and typically what you do best. Here are three strategies to hold space for your Big Rocks. Use these strategies alone or in combination based on what makes sense for you.

Strategy 1: Get Specific

Here are a few examples of specific Big Rock time blocks from me and my time management clients to get your wheels turning and inspire *your* Big Rock time blocks.

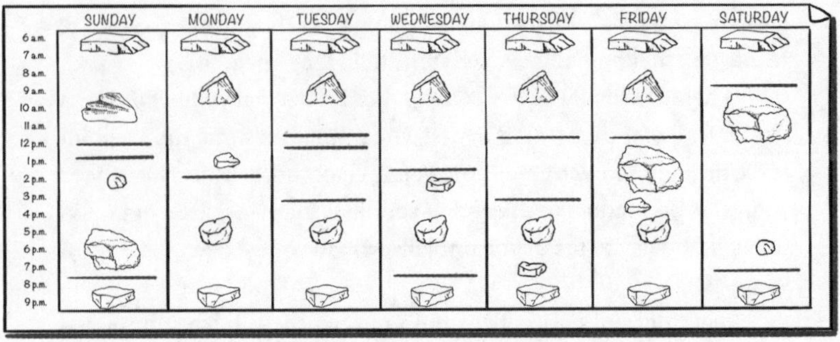

When I worked in crisis communications as a public relations account executive, every morning after I made a cup of coffee I settled in at my desk at 9:15 a.m. and spent an hour reading the latest news in each of my clients' industries. This was a proactive Big Rock for me because having my fingers on the pulse of their industries enabled me to be aware of media trends, opportunities, and potential obstacles.

As the communications manager at a museum, every Social Media Monday from 10 to 11 a.m., I walked the museum and snapped photos of pieces from our collection, new installations, and behind-the-scenes candids of our curatorial team at work.

As a congressional scheduler, every Friday from 9 to 11 a.m. was spent preparing the scheduling binder for review, and 1 to 3 p.m. was dedicated to scheduling and confirming meetings with constituents, lobbyists, and special interest groups.

Every Tuesday from 2 to 3 p.m., one of my clients blocks time for grant research prior to a standing client meeting during which an overview of grant research opportunities is on the agenda.

Strategy 2: Use Placeholders

Because Big Rocks are deadline-oriented and project-based, they aren't as steadfast as Boulders. They can change often. So instead of creating time blocks for ultra-specific Big Rock activities, consider creating Big Rock placeholders.

A past time management coaching client uses Big Rock placeholders in her Ideal Week to represent her three Big Rock projects at work. Project A has time blocks on Monday morning and afternoon. Project B has time blocks on Tuesday and Wednesday. Project C has a weekly time block on Thursdays. What she does during those time blocks changes from week to week based on the status of the project, but the placeholders remain steadfast. This enables her to carve out time every week to make progress on all three of her projects, instead of spending too much time on a single project and unintentionally neglecting the rest.

Similar to using placeholders for Big Rock projects, you can also create placeholders in your day for different types of work. For example, you could dedicate time blocks in the morning to work that requires more focus, such as writing or analytical decision-making. Then, you could dedicate time blocks in the afternoon to more low-impact work.

Strategy 3: Turn Your Pebbles into Big Rocks with Task Batches

Finally, we'll round out our Big Rock time blocking strategies by squeezing some of our Pebbles into Big Rocks using task batches. Carve out time in your schedule to handle task batches like email or communication, financial tasks, administrative to-dos, and any other task batches you've created.

Step 7: Sprinkle in the Pebbles

Now that you've blocked out your Big Rocks by creating specific time blocks, placeholders, or task batches, we're officially in the home stretch. All that's left is sprinkling in your Pebbles. Pebbles will inevitably need to be dealt with, even if you've eliminated, automated, and delegated most of the unimportant, nonurgent tasks in your life and work.

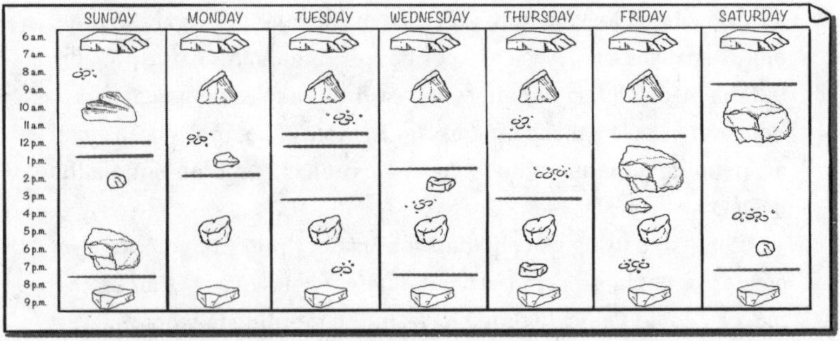

The great thing about most Pebble priorities is that they're small and can be squeezed in between the Boulders and Big Rocks. Another idea is to create a weekly Pebble Power Hour time block dedicated to knocking out all of the random Pebbles that have accumulated in the past week. Order a gift for that birthday party next weekend. Order more stamps. Make a doctor's appointment. Schedule a babysitter. When you give your Pebbles their own home in your Ideal Week, you're less likely to burn your productive time tackling them during other parts of your week.

Step 8: Review and Celebrate

First, give yourself major kudos for taking time to thoughtfully design your Ideal Week. Most people will never take the time to map out a detailed blueprint for their time, but you have!

Now that you've completed a first draft of your Ideal Week, start at the beginning and mentally walk through each day of your week. Is anything missing? Are all of your Boulders in place? Is there enough time carved out for your Big Rocks? Are your Values represented?

At this point, you might be looking at your Ideal Week and feeling some pretty intense satisfaction. You've got a place for everything and everything's in its place. Your Values are represented, and you've got time for your Boulders, Big Rocks, and Pebbles.

However, you might be looking at your Ideal Week and it feels impossible. You might even be frustrated, thinking: *Ugh! I just don't have enough time for everything I* need *to do, much less time for what I* want *to do!*

If you're in the second category and you're feeling frustrated, I want to encourage you. Yes, you have enough time. You have 168 hours in your week and the ability to control how you spend those hours.

If you're feeling frustrated or overwhelmed, walk away from your Ideal Week draft and come back to it later. If it still feels too full, or impossible, or that it's not an accurate reflection of how you'd like to spend your time, it may be time for a change. Ask yourself what you can cut, reduce, or rearrange in order to create the space you need.

Seeing your first attempt at an Ideal Week laid out in front of you might be the catalyst for taking a deeper dive into what you can eliminate, automate, and delegate in order to create more time for what matters most to you. Remember, the power is in the process, and designing your Ideal Week may be the first step to a transformation that might take some time but will be well worth it if it enables you to live your Vision and be true to your Values.

As you continue to refine your Ideal Week, I encourage you to keep your Values nearby and ask yourself if the time blocks on your calendar reflect your Values. Don't stop tweaking, adjusting, and rearranging until you can confidently say they do.

We don't have to wait until someday to start living our dream life. We don't have to wait until we have "more time" or "enough time" to live our Values. We really can start this week—today even! Yes, we *can* make time for what matters. You're already on your way.

HOW TO USE YOUR IDEAL WEEK

Having created your Ideal Week, you might be wondering what exactly you're supposed to *do* with it. First, remember that your Ideal Week is a planning and decision-making tool, not a measuring stick of perfection.

To get the most of your Ideal Week, use it to map out your week ahead. This is best done during a Weekly Planning Session, which we'll explore deeper in Chapter 7. If you exclusively use a paper planner, keep a copy of your Ideal Week bookmarked, tucked in a pocket, or taped in the inside cover. If you use a digital calendar, simply toggle your Ideal Week calendar into view and use it as a template each time you schedule your time blocks and make appointments for the week ahead. Remember, it's unlikely you'll ever execute your Ideal Week flawlessly, so go ahead and remove any pressure to get it perfect.

FREQUENTLY ASKED QUESTIONS

As you followed the step-by-step instructions for designing your Ideal Week, you might have encountered some questions that have you wondering whether an Ideal Week makes sense for you. Fortunately, there are many ways to customize your Ideal Week to fit your life. Here are answers to some common Ideal Week questions:

- **What if my real week never matches my Ideal Week?**
  It's worth reiterating that your Ideal Week isn't a measuring stick for perfection or success. It's a decision-making tool. By designing an Ideal Week, you've already made decisions about how you'd like to spend your week. Now, you can reduce your decision fatigue by making fewer decisions about how you'll spend your time in the moment because you've already made them!

- **How do I use my Ideal Week if the week ahead is not a typical week?**
  First, there's no such thing as a typical week. Rarely will you work 40 hours in a week without some type of variation from the norm. Nearly every week contains some kind of diversion from what you consider "typical." There will be a doctor's appointment. A kid will get sick. You'll have Monday off because of a holiday. A coworker will be unavailable, causing you to reschedule a meeting and adjust your project timeline.

  When you keep in mind that your Ideal Week is a *planning tool*, it gives you a model to reference and adapt for the week ahead. Maybe you won't be able to do everything you've planned in your Ideal Week during the week ahead, but because you've already mapped out what's most important, you'll be equipped to make more thoughtful decisions about what stays, what shifts, and what gets rescheduled.

- **What if my schedule isn't consistent week to week because it cycles?**
A cyclical schedule is common for many, and the solution is to create different versions of your Ideal Week to adapt. Here are a few examples of how you can use multiple Ideal Weeks to reflect the realities of your life.

As a time management coach, I utilize three Ideal Weeks to manage my time: a coaching week, a podcast week, and a program week. My 1:1 time management coaching sessions occur every other week. That means two weeks of my month are typically very meeting heavy with Tuesdays, Wednesdays, and Thursdays filled with back-to-back coaching sessions. That leaves two weeks to focus on other things. During podcast week, I write solo episodes and record guest interviews for my *It's About Time* podcast. During program week, I create content for the It's About Time Academy, build out new self-paced coaching programs, or prepare for upcoming speaking engagements or live workshops.

Having three Ideal Weeks adapts to that cycle (coaching, podcast, coaching, programs), creates consistency for me, and sets expectations with my team for what we'll focus on and when.

One of my It's About Time Academy members, Amy, also utilizes three Ideal Weeks. Amy is the full-time president of a real estate development company, the owner of a bag and accessory brand, and an officer in the Army National Guard. She's also a mom and a wife, and she's involved in her community. Needless to say, Amy has a lot on her plate.

Since Amy attends one Army National Guard drill weekend a month, she designed three different Ideal Weeks to meet the unique needs of each week: a Pre-Drill Ideal Week, a Post-Drill Ideal Week, and a No Drill Ideal Week.

Cycling two Ideal Weeks is also a helpful structure for parents who share parenting responsibilities. Creating an Ideal Week when your kids are home and creating a separate Ideal Week when your kids are away helps you establish rhythms and quickly adjust when kids leave and return.

- **What if a week isn't enough time to capture all of the things I need or want to do?**
  Some things just don't need to be done every week. Perhaps you offer a VIP day for clients only once a month. Maybe you schedule a monthly runaround day dedicated to batching all of your errands around town. Whatever your scenario, you may find that creating an Ideal Month is a better fit for you. Before you embark on your Ideal Month design, be sure to start with just an Ideal Week, or consider cycling two or three Ideal Weeks. Our goal is to keep things simple, and diving straight into designing an Ideal Month might be overwhelming. When things feel overwhelming, we're more likely to procrastinate, so start small and keep it simple before pursuing a full-blown Ideal Month.

- **How often should I update my Ideal Week?**
  Shifts in the seasons; kids heading back to school or being at home for the summer; adjusting to a new baby, a new job,

or any other events that change your routines—all are great opportunities to revamp your Ideal Week. Typically, you'll notice when your Ideal Week no longer feels like a good match for your reality.

Like most strategies in our time management toolbox, your Ideal Week isn't something that you can set and forget for long. It's most effective when you revisit it every few months to make sure that it still represents the best use of your time. Consider adding a reminder to your calendar each quarter to pause and reflect on the effectiveness of your Ideal Week. Then, make any adjustments that will help your Ideal Week serve as a better decision-making tool for how you spend your time.

ESSENTIAL TAKEAWAYS

- An Ideal Week is a template for how you'd like to spend your time each week. It's a decision-making tool that enables you to live your Values, make time for what matters most, and end each week feeling accomplished.
- To design your Ideal Week, create time blocks for your Boulder and Big Rock priorities on a blank calendar. Use the remaining space for Pebbles. Adjust, rearrange, and resize your time blocks until you've designed a week that fits your current season of life.
- You may find that utilizing multiple, situation-specific Ideal Weeks or designing an Ideal Month will best fit your life. Be sure to revisit your Ideal Week monthly or quarterly to ensure that it's still serving as an effective planning tool through life's changing seasons.

Win Your Week Before It Starts

As a time management coach, a common question I'm asked as a guest on podcasts or from workplace and wellness writers is: "What is one thing someone can do differently this week to improve their time management?" My answer is always the same. This chapter is dedicated to that one thing. It's dedicated to doing things differently, and it's called a Weekly Planning Session.

WEEKLY PLANNING SESSION

Where did the week go? It's Friday, and you're left with unfinished items on your to-do list, forgotten laundry, and regret from skipping the gym and eating fast-food meals because of an empty fridge. You keep thinking there has to be a better way, but you're not sure what that means or where you'd even find time to fix all of the problems scattered throughout the week.

The answer is that you don't solve them *during the week*. You solve them *before* they become problems at all—with a Weekly Planning Session.

A Weekly Planning Session is a block of time set aside each week, usually on the same day of the week, to look ahead and make decisions that will help your week move smoothly once it's in motion. It can be short and sweet, only 15–30 minutes, and yet it can give you back hours of your time.

THREE BENEFITS OF A WEEKLY PLANNING SESSION

A Weekly Planning Session is your bird's-eye view of the week ahead that enables you to make a lot of decisions at once, spot obstacles before they happen, identify potential solutions, catch communication breakdowns, and win your week before it starts.

Benefit 1: Get an Overview of the Week Ahead

When you carve out time for a Weekly Planning Session, you have a designated opportunity to zoom out and look at your entire week at once. When you only look at your calendar or your to-do list day by day, you're getting a narrow view of what's actually on your plate. But, look at the week as a whole and you can gauge the overall feeling of the week. Will this week feel frantic because you have an abundance of meetings, deadlines, and travel? Will this week feel rushed because your kids have lots of after-school activities? Will this week feel restful because you have a day off and no major project milestones? Plus, looking at your week ahead and using your Ideal Week from Chapter 6 as a guide enables you to create a realistic to-do list for each day. A more manageable to-do list increases your chances of ending each day, and the week as a whole, feeling content and accomplished.

Benefit 2: Combat Decision Fatigue

Every day, we make between 200 and 300 decisions just about food! It's no wonder we end each day and wrap each week feeling completely drained of our decision-making fuel. So, in addition to mapping out your time blocks for the week and creating a realistic to-do list, one of the biggest opportunities to decrease decision fatigue is to plan your meals in advance. What does your week look like? Will you bring lunch to work or take a potential client to lunch? Do you have a late meeting on Tuesday? That sounds like a great opportunity to have an Instant Pot recipe ready to go. Don't like cleaning up the kitchen on Sunday nights? Make Sunday a standing pizza night. With a Weekly Planning Session that includes mapping out your meals, you'll never be hangry again.

Beyond meal planning, there are many opportunities to plan in advance. Decide which mornings you'll meet a friend for coffee before work. Lay out your kids' clothes or sports gear the night before to make mornings easier and after-school activities less frantic. Coordinating travel, transportation, carpools, pet care, and more are all decisions that can be made in advance. The possibilities are endless and can be customized based on your unique roles and responsibilities.

If you have a flexible or hybrid working arrangement, decide which days you'll work remotely and which days you'll go to the office. One of my past workshop clients is a business owner with two small children. With a home office and company office space across town, she chooses her desk for the day based on her meeting schedule. Then, she coordinates additional childcare based on the days she heads into the office. Her Weekly Planning Session creates a domino effect of decision-making.

Benefit 3: Identify Obstacles, Find Solutions, and Catch Communication Breakdowns

A Weekly Planning Session helps you see into the future. I'm not talking about crystal balls or time travel, but when you zoom out and look at your week ahead all at once, you can identify potential trouble spots.

For example, you might realize you've accidentally double-booked yourself on Thursday. The dental appointment you scheduled six months ago is now at the exact time you're leading a meeting at work. When you notice this conflict during your Weekly Planning Session on Sunday, you can make a note to reschedule your dental appointment first thing Monday morning. Or you can shift the start time of the meeting. Whichever option you choose, you give everyone, including yourself, time to adjust.

Now imagine that you don't do a Weekly Planning Session, and instead take your week day by day. You don't realize until Wednesday, or even worse, Thursday morning, that you're double-booked. Now you've got to scramble to rearrange your schedule and wrestle with the consequences of how the last-minute shift affects others.

At our house, it's not uncommon for me to give an evening time management workshop to a professional organization or corporate employee resource group. During my Weekly Planning Session, I make sure to let my husband know when I have an evening event. I'll even send him a calendar invitation so he has a visible reminder to be available. That enables him to shift his schedule as needed so he can be prepared to handle the bath time and bedtime routines for our girls. It's one of our best methods for catching communication breakdowns *before* they happen.

A successful Weekly Planning Session isn't only about dodging problems. You can also use your weekly planning time to schedule some fun! When you look at the week ahead, you're able to make plans for the weekend that wouldn't be possible as a last-minute decision. You can decide to buy tickets to an event, make a reservation, schedule childcare, or plan a day trip. Cultivating relationships takes intention and setting aside time in your Weekly Planning Session to decide who you want to take to coffee this week, or when you'd like to have a happy hour with friends is another great way to use the time.

HOW TO DESIGN YOUR WEEKLY PLANNING SESSION

Now that you see how incredibly helpful a Weekly Planning Session can be, it's time to design yours.

There are four steps to designing a Weekly Planning Session. First, decide what you'll plan and create an agenda. Second, determine what tools you'll need to have nearby to be efficient with your time. Third, choose a recurring time for your Weekly Planning Session and schedule it in your calendar. Fourth, decide how you'll make your planning session fun so you're more likely to stick with it week after week.

Let's dive deeper into each step.

Step 1: Decide What You'll Plan and Create an Agenda

Have you ever attended a meeting that didn't have an agenda? I think we can agree that's basically the worst. Meetings without agendas are a terrible use of our limited time, focus, and resources because they lack direction and purpose.

A Weekly Planning Session with no agenda can be just as worthless. If you're going to plan your week effectively, you've got to have a plan for planning your week. What is it that you need to plan in order to have a smooth week? What decisions can you make in advance so you're not caught off guard and forced to make a decision in the moment, a moment when you may not be at your best?

When you have a clear step-by-step plan for your Weekly Planning Session, your very own agenda, you're more likely to think through all of the potential obstacles that could come your way. When you identify potential obstacles, you're more effective at devising solutions and creating realistic to-do lists. When you've got solutions in your back pocket and manageable to-do lists to follow each day, you're more likely to end your week feeling accomplished and proud. And when you end your week feeling great, you create a chain reaction of momentum and positive feelings heading into the next week.

To create your Weekly Planning Session agenda, open your calendar to a recent week and mentally walk through your week day by day. What decisions could you have made in advance? Where are your opportunities to batch tasks instead of scattering them throughout the week? What decisions are you making every day that could be made at the beginning of the week? Create your brainstorm list, and use these ideas as inspiration:

- Time block your Boulders, Big Rocks, and Pebbles
- Plan your meals
- Make your grocery list
- Submit your grocery order
- Review your budget
- Categorize your expenses
- Review your goals
- Plan your workouts
- Reserve your spot in workout classes
- Make travel arrangements
- Map out your commute time
- Finalize childcare
- Choose your outfits for the week
- Choose your kids' outfits for the week
- Review upcoming work deadlines
- Check the status of current home projects
- Schedule a coffee date with a friend
- Finalize weekend plans
- Update your reading list
- Print photos from your camera roll

- Prep birthday or anniversary cards
- Write thank you notes

Once you've created your brainstorm list, put your list in order based on the flow that makes sense. Which domino needs to fall first in order to tip the next and the next? For example, you could first review your calendar, then plan your meals, and then make your grocery list.

Here's a sample agenda for a Weekly Planning Session:

1. Review your calendar and note any appointments that require transition time or prep work.
2. Using your Ideal Week as a guide, add time blocks for your Boulders, Big Rocks, and Pebbles.
3. Identify your tough spots. Where are the conflicts or tight time frames? When are you most likely to be tired or stressed?
4. Devise potential solutions to those tough spots.
5. Plan your meals.
6. Make your grocery list.
7. Check the weather.
8. Choose your clothing for the week.

When you have an agenda for your Weekly Planning Session and follow it in the same order every time, eventually you won't even need your agenda because it's become an ingrained habit. Until then, write down your agenda step-by-step and follow it in order to strengthen your weekly planning muscle and build your planning habit.

Step 2: Decide What Tools You Need

One of my annual holiday traditions is a marathon baking session. Instead of dozens of Christmas cookies or yummy holiday candy, I bake the Big White Cake on the cover of the December issue of *Southern Living* magazine. Baking this delicious showstopper is no simple task. The instructions are tedious, some of the ingredients are unusual and difficult to find, and the entire process from start to finish can take several days.

My first attempt at baking the Big White Cake was a bit of a disaster. I naively thought I could prop open the pages of the magazine, read the recipe, and pull ingredients from my pantry as needed. After multiple trips to the grocery store and a lot of wasted time, I learned my lesson. As it turns out, one of the most important parts of the baking process begins before you preheat the oven.

Mise en place is a French culinary term that means "putting in place." It involves gathering all of the ingredients in advance, measuring them out, and setting out all of the necessary spatulas, spoons, bowls, and anything else I need to have at my fingertips to bring the Big White Cake to life. This makes baking quicker, easier, and much more successful.

Your Weekly Planning Session needs its own *mise en place*. If you sit down to do your Weekly Planning Session and realize you don't have your fitness program's meal plan handy, you'll get up and walk across the house to find it. That opens up the possibility you'll be distracted along the way. Maybe you'll stop to refill the dog bowl, get your kid a snack, or move the laundry from the washer to the dryer. The next thing you know, it's two hours later and you've completely forgotten about your Weekly Planning Session!

Create your own "mise en place" for your Weekly Planning Session.

When you've got everything you need *before* you sit down to start planning, you're setting yourself up for success by making your planning session easy. Create your own Weekly Planning Session *mise en place* by looking at the agenda you created in step 1. Ask yourself: *What do I need to have on hand to successfully make decisions about each of these agenda items?* If you review your goals, you may want to have your goal planner. If you're participating in a fitness program with a specific meal plan, make sure you have those resources ready. If your kids are in multiple activities with different schedules, grab those, too.

To make your *mise en place* easy to gather each week, consider keeping all of your weekly planning tools in a special place. Maybe that's an extra tote bag where your weekly planning tools live each week. Whatever you choose, make sure your tools are together, organized, and easy to travel with just in case you decide to or need to change your planning spot.

This suggestion might seem fairly obvious, but you'll want your calendar—whether it's digital or paper—close by, too.

Step 3: Decide When to Do Your Weekly Planning Session

There are no rules when it comes to when you do your Weekly Planning Session, but your planning session will be most effective when it's consistent.

Planning on a Sunday, and then a Thursday, and then a Tuesday isn't going to give you the same picture of your week ahead. Instead, do your Weekly Planning Session on the same day each week. I've found that Sunday is a popular day for weekly planning, but many have success holding a Weekly Planning Session on a Friday afternoon or first thing Monday morning.

If you're new to weekly planning, start with Sunday and then test-drive different options to find the best time for you and the rhythm of your life. Regardless of when you choose, it's important to set a date and time. "Someday," "at some point this weekend," and "when I have some free time" are not going to magically appear for you.

Another tip? Put your Weekly Planning Session into your Ideal Week with a time block. This will ensure you've always got space held for it. Your Weekly Planning Session is a routine that helps you be your best self, so it definitely falls in the Boulder category.

Step 4: Decide How You'll Make It Fun

Oh yes, we're building *fun* into our Weekly Planning Session. Our goal is to make doing a Weekly Planning Session a habit, something you do automatically. It helps to know that there are three building blocks of a habit: the cue, the routine, and the reward. The cue is the circumstance that triggers the habit. The routine is the habit itself, and the reward is how you feel afterward. Using a Weekly Planning Session as an example, a cue could be a reminder notification from your calendar that it's time to start your Weekly Planning Session. The routine is doing your Weekly Planning Session. The reward is the calm and prepared feeling you have when you complete your planning session.

Whenever you're starting a new habit, sometimes you may not feel the reward or the intrinsic benefits immediately. It can take a few weeks to get into a groove and experience the results of planning in advance. When you don't feel an immediate reward for your hard work, it's easier to give up. That's where planning for fun comes in.

When you plan a reward or pair a fun activity with your Weekly Planning Session, you'll have something to look forward to and you'll be more likely to follow through with your session as planned. The reward, whether it's getting a fancy coffee or lighting your favorite candle, will tell your brain that Weekly Planning Sessions are a good thing and that you should keep doing them! This external reward tides you over until the intrinsic reward kicks in, thus solidifying your Weekly Planning Session as a habit.

Here are other ideas for making your Weekly Planning Session fun, but don't limit yourself to just these:

- Head outside and plan in a park.
- Schedule something fun right after.
- Listen to relaxing music.
- Pour and enjoy a glass of wine.
- Meet a friend and plan together.
- Indulge in a sweet treat.

WEEKLY PLANNING SESSION WHAT IFS

If there's one thing we've all learned from the past few years, it's that life can throw us a curveball at any moment. That's why a Weekly Planning Session is such a valuable use of your time. When life gets thrown off track, your Weekly Planning Session is dedicated time to get a game plan, pivot, and keep making progress in the direction of your Vision while staying true to your Values and honoring your priorities. Here are a few common Weekly Planning Session questions that might be on your mind:

- **What if life throws a curveball and I don't have time to do my Weekly Planning Session this week?**
  It certainly happens. Kids get sick. You get sick. There's an emergency at work. There are a multitude of challenges that can disrupt your weekly planning time. Before this happens, think through and identify your "bare minimum" Weekly Planning Session. If you only have time for one thing on your agenda, what is that one thing? What are the most important things that must be planned in advance to ensure that your week goes smoothly?

  At our house, the bare minimum looks like quickly reviewing my calendar for evening obligations, meal planning, making a grocery order, and choosing Monday's school outfit for our girls. If we can manage to do those things, we can step into the week feeling ready, and then catch up on anything we missed later in the week.

  Your Weekly Planning Session doesn't have to be all or nothing. Something, *anything*, is better than nothing. Oh, and don't forget to cut yourself some slack on the weeks when you have to do just the bare minimum. We've all been there, and you're doing your best.

- **What if I can't do my entire Weekly Planning Session agenda all in one sitting? If I break it into smaller parts, will it still be effective?**
  Before breaking your Weekly Planning Session into smaller sections, review your agenda and make sure you're not overloading yourself. When you're new to weekly planning, it can be exciting to think of all the things you can plan in advance. But if you try to do too much, you can quickly get overwhelmed and want to give up entirely!
  That said, there's nothing wrong with splitting your Weekly Planning Session into different parts if that's what works best with the rhythm of your life. You may want to do half of your agenda in the morning and the rest in the evening. For example, I consider picking out my daughters' school clothes for the week to be a part of my Weekly Planning Session, but I don't necessarily do that when I plan our meetings and obligations for the week. Instead, I pop into their rooms whenever I have a spare moment that day. Don't be afraid to try out different methods and find what works best for you.
- **What if I want to zoom out and look at my month? Could I do a single monthly planning session instead of Weekly Planning Sessions?**
  It seems that if a Weekly Planning Session is good, then a monthly planning session must be even better, right? Not

exactly. A monthly planning session is great to get a bird's-eye view of the month, but a lot can change between Day 1 and Day 31. Weekly planning makes it easier for you to adapt when—not if—things change.

That being said, monthly planning can work well *in addition* to weekly planning if you travel often and need to make reservations or coordinate transportation in advance. Monthly meal planning can also be a great method for cutting back on your grocery bills and introducing more variety into your weekly menus. When you plan on a weekly basis, it can be easy to get stuck in a rut of repeating the same dishes.

There may be certain aspects of your life that are well-served with a monthly planning session, but a *single* monthly planning session isn't a substitute for a recurring Weekly Planning Session.

• • •

Whether you use your Weekly Planning Session to plan for work, life, or a combination of both, you'll quickly feel the benefits of your advance decision-making. You'll feel more prepared for meetings, more present in your downtime, and more accomplished at the end of each week. When you know what you'll plan, identify what planning tools to have readily available, set a consistent planning rhythm, and inject some fun, you're on your way to winning each week before it starts.

ESSENTIAL TAKEAWAYS

- A Weekly Planning Session is your bird's-eye view of the week ahead that enables you to make a lot of decisions at once, spot obstacles before they happen, identify potential solutions, catch communication breakdowns, and win your week before it starts.
- To design a successful Weekly Planning Session, decide what you'll plan, identify what tools you need to plan, schedule your planning session in your calendar, and decide how you'll make your planning session fun.
- There are a multitude of challenges that can disrupt your weekly planning time. Before this happens, identify the one or two most important things that must be planned in advance to ensure your week goes smoothly. Then focus your limited time and attention on that short list.

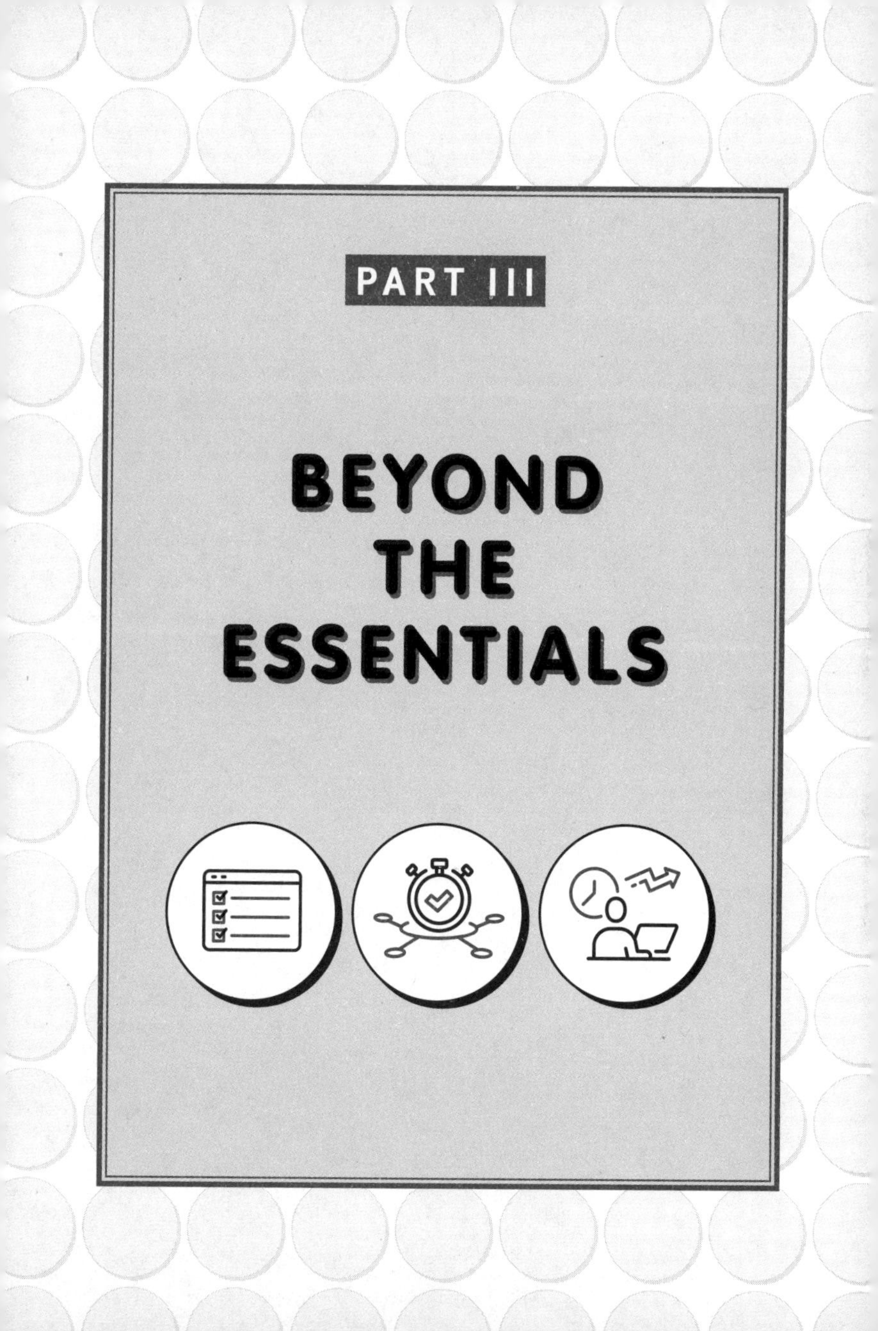

PART III

BEYOND THE ESSENTIALS

Get Mentally Organized

"A place for everything and everything in its place."

As a teenager, it was common for me to hear this reminder from my mother as she'd walk into my slightly cluttered, but never completely messy bedroom. Sure, there were times I couldn't find my car keys, my pom poms, the red shorts I needed for dance practice, or the permission slip that needed to be signed, but for the most part, I kept things in order.

Now that I'm a full-fledged adult with a business and my own children who need permission slips signed, "a place for everything and everything in its place" is a mantra I definitely get behind. But now, instead of just organizing physical clutter and finding my car keys, it's managing mental clutter that requires the greatest effort.

MENTAL CLUTTER

Mental clutter. It's that all too common feeling of being overwhelmed we experience when we're trying to remember too many things and keep track of too many important pieces of information in our heads. Also known as cognitive overload, it's constantly worrying that you're going to forget something, as if there are too many browser tabs open in your brain and they're constantly refreshing. When we're feeling mentally overwhelmed, we make more mistakes, struggle to stay focused, and are more prone to anxiety and procrastination.

In an effort to reduce your mental load, you might commit to writing down every thought and to-do that pops into your head. Yet you can't remember where you put that sticky note from yesterday, or which notebook you used to write down the updated deadlines for that project. Soon, we feel like we're failing because we can't keep track of it all. We worry we're starting to lose our minds since we can never remember everything. When it comes to mental clutter, your mind feels a bit like a filing cabinet, but instead of neatly alphabetized files in color-coded folders, everything is just sort of piled in with no rhythm or reason, making recalling that information near impossible. That's information overload in full effect.

If this sounds familiar, you're not alone. And if this sounds like a hopeless situation, it's not. But what exactly does organizing mental clutter look like? How do we sort through a pile of thoughts? It's not as if Marie Kondo, author of *The Life-Changing Magic of Tidying Up*, can hop inside through your brain and help you figure out what sparks joy. *The Home Edit*'s Clea Shearer and Joanna Teplin can't exactly organize your thoughts inside clear plastic bins.

When your most important information is organized and easily accessible, you can give your brain a break. Instead of trying to keep track of #allthethings, your energy can go toward decision-making, planning, making progress on your big dreams, and just enjoying life.

FOUR TOOLS TO CUT MENTAL CLUTTER

There are four types of tools that every Purpose-driven professional needs to get organized and keep mental clutter in check. That toolbox includes a digital dashboard, as well as tools for managing your calendar, capturing ideas, and collaborating with others. In this chapter, we'll explore each of these types of tools, how to use them to organize your life and work, and how to choose the tools that work in *your* toolbox.

Your Digital Dashboard

A minute here . . . a few minutes there. The time we spend searching for information may seem insignificant in the moment, but it adds up. In fact, the average employee spends more than 3.5 hours a day just searching for information![1] All of that searching can leave us feeling frustrated and exhausted, and it can cause us to fall behind on our work. That's why a digital dashboard with your most searched information is a mental clutter-busting, time-saving tool in your Purpose-driven productivity toolbox.

A digital dashboard can organize and store your most frequently referenced information. Think of it as creating a "Frequently Asked Questions" guide for yourself. A place for your Employer Identification Number, your business address, your brand color hex codes, and more—your digital dashboard is a one-stop resource for those pieces of information you find yourself searching for regularly.

When your most important information is at your fingertips in a digital dashboard, you spend less time searching for information and more time on high-impact work. A digital dashboard also decreases your mental load. Instead of trying to remember key pieces of information, or where that information is saved, you can rely on your digital dashboard to remember it for you—and quickly.

Here are three simple steps to creating your own digital dashboard.

Step 1: Decide What Belongs on Your Digital Dashboard

First, begin by deciding what information goes on your digital dashboard. Pay attention to information that you search for during the week. When you frequently search for a piece of information, add it to your digital dashboard list.

Step 2: Decide Where Your Digital Dashboard Will Live

Now that you've created the list of items you want on your digital dashboard, decide where your dashboard will live. The ideal digital dashboard can be easily organized, referenced, and updated. Your digital dashboard also should be easily accessible from multiple devices. This increases its convenience, especially if you work from multiple locations, you want to share this dashboard with others, you have several people contributing to it, you travel for work, or you're often on the go.

While there are many tools and programs that could serve as your digital dashboard, a few of my favorites include Trello, Asana, and Notion. A Google Doc or a Google Sheet can also work well. Although it can be tempting to house all of your frequently searched information in a binder, I encourage you to use a digital platform.

A paper reference guide isn't searchable, nor is it easy to update. A digital platform enables you to quickly access and update your information when it changes so you're not accidentally referencing outdated information.

Step 3: Fill in Your Digital Dashboard

Once you've chosen your digital dashboard platform, fill in the details. Create a time block in your calendar dedicated to entering in the information for each item on the list from step 1. Although creating the dashboard and filling in this information may take a few hours, it will save you time moving forward.

If you're unable to block out several consecutive hours to fill in your complete digital dashboard, block out multiple 30-minute time blocks each week to enter your information. Little by little, you'll build a comprehensive, easily referenced dashboard of information.

• • •

In addition to collecting your most frequently accessed work information in a digital dashboard, you can create dashboards for your personal life, or even specific projects. For example, one of my time management coaching clients created a dashboard to keep track of the details for the construction of her new home. From contractor contact information to paint colors, fixtures, and more, her digital dashboard was easily accessed from her computer at home, her phone at the construction site, or her iPad while shopping in home decor stores.

Your Calendar Tool

It should come as no surprise that a time management coach writing about time management is going to advocate that you have a calendar.

To manage your time well, you've got to have a consistent place to plan ahead and keep track of your appointments and time blocks.

My recommended calendar tool is a digital calendar. While there will always be a special place in my heart for a paper planner, it's my observation that for individuals managing a large number of appointments across personal, professional, and family schedules, a paper planner alone is not nimble enough to keep up with the speed of life. However, a paper planner can be productive as a *companion* to a digital calendar to keep day-to-day time blocks and to-dos.

With everything you've learned in this book, you're now a calendar expert, so we'll move on to the next tool you need in your Purpose-driven productivity toolbox.

Your Capture Tools

Ever feel like your brain is moving a mile a minute? That's probably because healthy adults process an average of 6,200 thoughts each day.[2] We're constantly making mental connections, coming up with ideas, and thinking about things we need to do. But the reality of life is that we can't act on every single idea we have the moment we have it. Sometimes you remember while you're grocery shopping that you need a dinner reservation for your upcoming anniversary. Sometimes while you're focused on an intense work project you remember that you need to follow up with a colleague on the status of a different project. And some of our best light bulb moments happen while we're in the shower!

One of the biggest mistakes we can make when it comes to productivity is attempting to act on our ideas the moment we have them. We think *I need to check in with Steve about the Jones project. I don't want to forget, so let me just do that right now.* The next thing we know, we've lost our lost our focus on the project in front of us, halted our progress, and kicked off a journey down a rabbit hole of context switching.

So, what do we do with the ideas we shouldn't act on right now but don't want to forget? This is where a capture tool saves the day.

Simply put, a capture tool is a dedicated space for capturing ideas and information. Capture tools can take many forms. While a sticky note and an online task management system are both examples of capture tools, some tools are more effective at capturing your ideas and to-dos in a way that keeps them easily organized and accessible when you need them. One important clarification? Your to-do list is *not* a capture tool. Instead, the notepad, journal, app, or scraps of paper where you keep your to-do list is your actual capture tool.

In most cases, it's beneficial to have at least three capture tools. A high-tech capture tool, a low-tech capture tool, and a physical inbox. I'll dive into what these are and why each type is helpful in an exercise. But first, here are three simple steps to choosing your capture tools.

Step 1: Choose a High-Tech Capture Tool

A high-tech capture tool is similar to your digital dashboard in that it's searchable, cloud-based, and easily shared with others. While your digital dashboard and your high-tech capture tool have a lot in common, there is a difference. Your digital dashboard is where you store your frequently referenced pieces of information. Your high-tech capture tool, on the other hand, is where you capture and organize your thoughts, ideas, meeting notes, goals, and other pieces of information in order to act on them later. An effective high-tech capture tool can be accessed from anywhere, such as a desktop version and a mobile or app version.

High-tech capture tools include online project management systems like Trello, Asana, and Notion. Evernote, Google Docs, and

Google Keep are also commonly used to capture ideas and notes. Because there are so many options available, one potential time-wasting trap is searching for the perfect tool. Every available tool will have pros and cons associated with its user experience and available features. So go ahead and pick a tool and stick with it.

Step 2: Choose a Low-Tech Capture Tool

Sometimes it's just not convenient to whip out your laptop or smartphone to capture your latest idea before it's gone. That's why it's helpful to have a low-tech capture tool. A notebook, journal, or legal pad can fill this role. When you choose your low-tech capture tool make sure it's appropriately sized. While tossing a mini-notebook in your bag might be convenient, if you have large handwriting you will be frustrated trying to fit your ideas on a tiny page.

A common pitfall when choosing a low-tech capture tool is choosing too many! Although having a separate notebook for each school subject was the norm in our younger years, having 15 different notebooks is a recipe for confusion and feeling overwhelmed. Instead of reaping the benefits of a streamlined system, with too many tools, you'll find yourself scrambling to figure out which notebook contains which ideas. Just like your high-tech capture tool, pick one low-tech tool and stick with it.

Step 3: Choose a Physical Inbox

Although many of our important documents are digital, we still have paper to deal with in the form of mail, notes from our kids' school, insurance documents, bills, and more. If you're tired of the pile of stuff on your kitchen counter or desk, a physical inbox can bring order to the chaos.

Pick up a document tray, a wall pocket, or even an empty box and designate that space as your physical inbox. Instead of chasing down assorted papers that have landed in various spots around the house or in your office, corral it all in your physical inbox. Instead of acting on each piece of paper in the moment, incorporate emptying the inbox and processing the papers into your daily shutdown routine or your weekly wrap-up routine.

• • •

Choosing your three capture tools doesn't mean you never use sticky notes or notepads ever again. But a layer of 37 sticky notes strewn across your desk dating back multiple weeks isn't a capture system. It's chaos. Whatever system you choose, make sure you transfer what you've captured on those sticky notes to your high-tech or low-tech capture tool. Or move that sticky note to your physical inbox so you can take action on it when you're ready.

Your Collaboration Tools

Remember my client in Chapter 2 with the convoluted email labeling system that included aToday and zUrgent? In addition to an overflowing inbox, she was also experiencing collaboration overload. Her unread email number continued to climb as her Slack messages piled up and her smartphone vibrated with new text messages. In an effort to be more accessible to her team, she became *too* accessible. She was drowning in communication and requests for collaboration. What's worse is that when her team didn't get a response via email, they sent her a Slack message. When they didn't hear from her on Slack, they sent a text. As a result, she was stuck in a constant cycle of checking (often duplicate) messages, moving from platform to platform and then starting over again. The solution to the chaos? A streamlined set of collaboration tools, each with its own specific purpose.

A collaboration tool is any tool you use to collaborate with others. Examples include Slack or Microsoft Teams, email, text messages, and even the comment functions in your project management systems. Using too many different tools to collaborate can be overwhelming because the likelihood of context switching is higher as you transition between tools. Like my client, you spend all your time moving between apps and checking messages to ensure you're up to date, but all of this "checking" time means less time actually engaged in meaningful work—plus more opportunities to make mistakes or have details fall through the cracks.

If you are experiencing communication overwhelm, or you want to stop it before it becomes a problem, there are three simple steps to clean up the chaos and create a collection of collaboration tools.

Step 1: List Tools You're Currently Using for Collaboration

Any tool that involves sending or receiving messages should be on the list, including email and text messages. If you have multiple email accounts, list them separately.

Step 2: Decide the Best Use of Each Tool

Next to each existing collaboration tool on your list, write down what you believe to be the *best* use of each tool. Keep in mind that the best use is not necessarily the *current* use of the tool. For example, your colleagues and clients may currently use text messages to communicate about work projects, but you might believe that text messages are best for personal communication. As you're noting the best use of each tool, you may realize that there are opportunities to streamline your tools by eliminating some of them.

Step 3: Define How to Use Each Tool Moving Forward

Going back to your list, decide the purpose of each collaboration tool in your collection. Perhaps Slack messages are the best for project status updates, text messages are off-limits to your colleagues and clients, and email is best for longer messages that require documentation. When each collaboration tool has a clear purpose, you can communicate that purpose to colleagues and clients. You can even create a collaboration standards guide that you share with your team that communicates the purpose and use cases of each tool on the list. When everyone on your team is operating within the same guidelines, you eliminate many questions, combat confusion, and reduce the time spent in the message-checking cyclone.

Our primary means of communication. Unless something falls in one of the other categories, please use email.

Instant Messaging

Used to send messages that are casual, transient, or timely.

Do not communicate over text. If you receive a text, direct the person to reach out over email.

Phone Calls

Best to be scheduled so the time is convenient for all parties. Can also be used if a matter is urgent and can be solved quickly with a conversation.

Used to assign tasks and manage projects.

YOUR PURPOSE-DRIVEN PRODUCTIVITY TOOLBOX

As we close this chapter, did you notice that each of the tools in your productivity toolbox should have a specific purpose and a set of guidelines or rules for its use? These rules aren't meant to be restrictive. Instead, they ensure there's clarity around what tool you use to do what, when you use each tool, and why you use that tool.

When you have organization systems set up, you'll experience less distractions and have more time to focus. You'll spend less time looking for the things you need to do your work, and more time getting things done. You'll feel less scatterbrained, because you know that everything has a place. Organizational systems not only save your sanity at work, they help you feel calm, prepared, and present in all areas of your life.

ESSENTIAL TAKEAWAYS

- Mental clutter is the feeling we have when trying to keep track of too much information in our heads.
- The four types of tools that everyone needs for Purpose-driven productivity are a digital dashboard, a calendar tool, capture tools, and collaboration tools.
- A digital dashboard is a place to organize and store your most frequently referenced information. A calendar tool is a consistent place to plan ahead and keep track of your appointments and time blocks. A capture tool is a dedicated space for capturing ideas and information. A collaboration tool is any tool you use to collaborate with others.
- Each tool in your productivity toolbox should have a specific purpose and set of guidelines for its use.

Get Energized

How many hours of work per week does it take to change the world? If you ask business magnate Elon Musk, the answer is between 80 and 100 hours.[1]

Before you open your Ideal Week to reconfigure your working time blocks to meet the 100-hour mark, let me stop you. Musk's recommendation fails to consider the law of diminishing returns, combined with the fluctuating energy levels that come with being human. We are not robots; we have limits.

Studies have shown that when people work more than 40 hours a week, their productive output begins to decline. The more hours you work after crossing the 40-hour mark, the less productive you actually are. Our productivity and precision are driven by our energy. If you're tired, you're just not going to be as effective as you could be. Instead of changing the world, 80 to 100 hours of work each week is more likely to land you in the hospital for burnout and exhaustion.

All hours in the day are not created equal. This is something I confirmed through self-experimentation while writing this book. As I'm typing these words, it's 10:04 p.m. and I'm feeling a bit sluggish. My eyes are tired, I'm not firing on all cylinders, and I notice that I'm frequently tapping the backspace key because I'm making more errors than usual. It's fair to say that I am *not* operating at my highest potential at this hour. It's a stark contrast to earlier this morning at 11 a.m. when I felt more alert, words came easy, and my typing finesse would have made my ninth-grade keyboarding teacher beam with pride.

Every hour of your day brings a different level of energy, focus, and stamina. Once you understand your own rhythms and how to harness your energy by paying attention to energy ebbs and flows throughout the day, you can take your time management to the next level. Imagine knowing exactly when to do the right work at the right time, skyrocketing your productivity. That's energy management meets time management.

When we think of energy, we tend to think of our natural energy levels. We know we feel alert at some points during the day and slow-moving and tired at others. However, there's more to the energy equation. In this chapter, we'll look at energy through two different lenses: your natural energy and your most energizing work. First, we'll explore the three energy phases and identify your unique biological chronotype. Then, we'll reveal the most energizing tasks on your to-do list by discovering what's in your Genius Zone (in addition to four other zones). Plus, you'll learn how to pair your most energizing work with your most energized hours of the day in order to optimize your productivity like never before.

WHAT ARE YOUR BEST HOURS?

Sometimes you're up; sometimes you're down. Maybe you're on fire in the mornings. Or perhaps you come alive in the evenings. We're all biologically wired to experience energy highs and lows throughout the day. In fact, there are three different energy phases that we all experience each day: the peak, the trough, and the rebound.

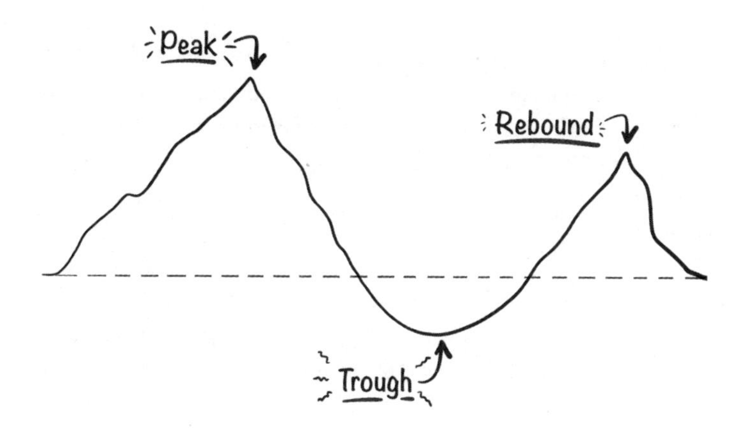

The *peak*, sometimes called your biological peak time, is your highest energy point in the day. This is when you feel amazing, and this is your best time for focused work that requires deep concentration. The peak is your most valuable time of day, and doing your most important work during your natural peak energy time will yield better results. You'll be faster, more focused, and more accurate with your work.

Since your peak is when you're at your best, guard this time as much as possible. Once you identify your peak hours, set aside this time to tackle your most important Big Rocks. Practice saying no to things that pop up during your peak time, and use this as an opportunity to shift meetings to lower energy times of your day.

The *trough* is your lowest energy point in the day, when your natural energy level tanks. Commonly occurring after lunchtime, this is when you're totally dragging and craving a coffee, a nap, or both. If you've ever felt the afternoon sleepies while trying to stay focused during a meeting, or you've struggled to stay focused while working through a dense report after lunch, you're trudging through your trough.

Brainstorming meetings are a strategic way to spend your trough time. The energy dip lowers our inhibitions and makes us more likely to share creative solutions that we might not when we're more alert. Repetitive administrative work like writing thank you notes, addressing envelopes, doing data entry, and anything that doesn't require intense focus are great ways to be productive during your trough. Best of all, if you can take a break during your trough time, do it. Sometimes the most productive thing you can do is take a break instead of trudging through a difficult, thought-intensive project with your lowest energy level. It's best to hold off focus work until your next peak or rebound time if you can.

The *rebound* is another high energy point, just not quite as high as your peak. Think of your rebound as a lite version of your peak. You're able to get stuff done, you're able to focus, and you feel pretty good.

Your rebound is the second wind that many of us feel as we're wrapping things up for the day. Like your peak, save important work for this time of day. Use your rebound for planning, or for tying up any loose ends.

YOUR BIOLOGICAL CHRONOTYPE

Another great way to manage your energy is to understand your biological chronotype. Even though we all experience three energy phases each and every day, we don't all experience them in the same order, or even at the same times of day! That's why knowing your unique biological chronotype is key to factoring your energy into your time management.

Before diving into biological chronotypes, it helps to understand the basics of sleep cycles and your body's internal clock, or circadian rhythms. Circadian rhythms are the 24-hour cycles that exist to make sure the body's processes are optimized throughout the day. Your circadian rhythm is influenced by a number of environmental cues, particularly light. Scrolling your phone right before bed and being exposed to the blue light glowing from the screen can disrupt your circadian rhythm and make it tougher to fall asleep. Although your circadian rhythm is mostly consistent throughout your life, it can be disrupted due to things like jet lag, prolonged night shift work, and certain sleep disorders.

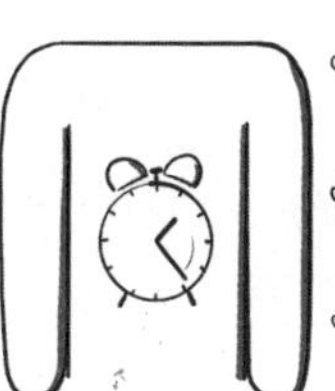

- 24-hour cycles
- Ensure bodily processes are optimized
- Mostly consistent throughout your life
- Influenced by a number of environmental cues
- Can be disrupted by light, jet lag, night shift work, certain sleep disorders, etc.

With that information in mind, your biological chronotype is your unique pattern of circadian rhythms that influence your sleep and wake times. Your chronotype impacts when you feel alert and when you feel tired. Knowing your biological chronotype lets you create a schedule that syncs with the energy ebbs and flows of your day. You can plan better, be more productive, and use your energy to your advantage when making decisions.

Usually biological chronotypes bring to mind two extremes: night owls and morning larks. Night owls stay up late to burn the midnight oil and then sleep late the next morning. Morning larks inspire thoughts of chirpy early birds, up before sunrise and turning to bed early. But what about the middle ground? If you don't identify with the night owls or morning larks, you're not alone.

Daniel H. Pink's Larks, Owls, and Third Birds

In his book *When: The Scientific Secrets of Perfect Timing,* Daniel H. Pink describes the already well-known duo, the morning lark and the night owl, and then adds the "third bird" to the mix. We'll use Pink's feathered trio to dive deeper into energy management.

Larks are our morning people. They're early to bed and early to rise. Owls are naturally late to bed and naturally late to rise. Third birds are those who don't fall squarely into the lark or owl categories. They rise early, but not as early as larks. They have energy in the evenings, but not as much as owls. Third birds are the most common type and make up about 60 to 80 percent of the population.[2]

Identifying Your Biological Chronotype

You likely have a pretty good idea of which of the three birds you are, but if you're not quite sure, here's a quick math problem.

Imagine it's your day off, and you have a totally free day. No obligations. No meetings. No parties or events. You don't even have to clean the house. You can literally do whatever you choose. Because your calendar is clear and you're free from all responsibilities, you can wake up whenever you choose. Turn off your alarm, because you can wake up naturally. And, surprise—you have another free day tomorrow, too.

Based on that scenario, what time would you choose to go to sleep the night before? Remember, you have no obligations and can head to bed whenever your body feels like it. Second, what time would you wake up that morning if you let yourself wake up naturally? Finally, what's the midpoint of those two times? For example, if you choose to go to bed around 11:30 p.m. and you'd wake up naturally at 7:30 a.m., your midpoint is 3:30 a.m.

As Pink explains in *When,* if your midpoint falls between midnight and 3:59 a.m., you're likely a morning lark. If your midpoint falls between 4 a.m. and 5:59 a.m., you're probably a third bird. If your midpoint falls between 6 a.m. and noon, chances are you're an owl.[3]

Understanding Your Unique Energy Pattern

Now that you know which feathered friend is your biological chronotype counterpart, use your unique energy pattern to plan your days. Some times of day are going to be more ideal for high concentration tasks. Other times will be best for taking a break. Not surprisingly, larks, owls, and third birds experience the three daily energy phases differently.

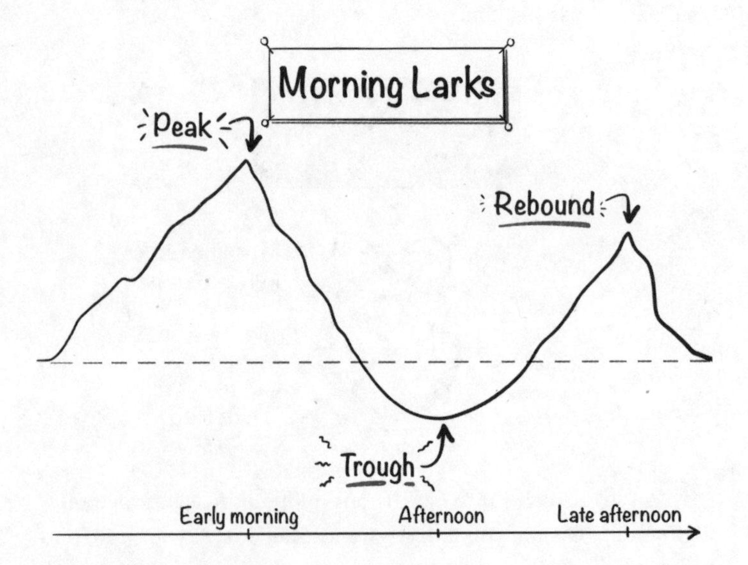

Larks experience the day in this order: peak, trough, rebound. They feel their peak in the early morning hours, experience their lowest point in the afternoon, and rebound in the late afternoon/early evening. Third birds experience the day in the same order as larks: peak, trough, rebound. However, third birds tend to start a bit later and experience their highest natural energy levels from early morning to mid-morning. Their energy dips in the afternoon, rebounding in the late afternoon/early evening.

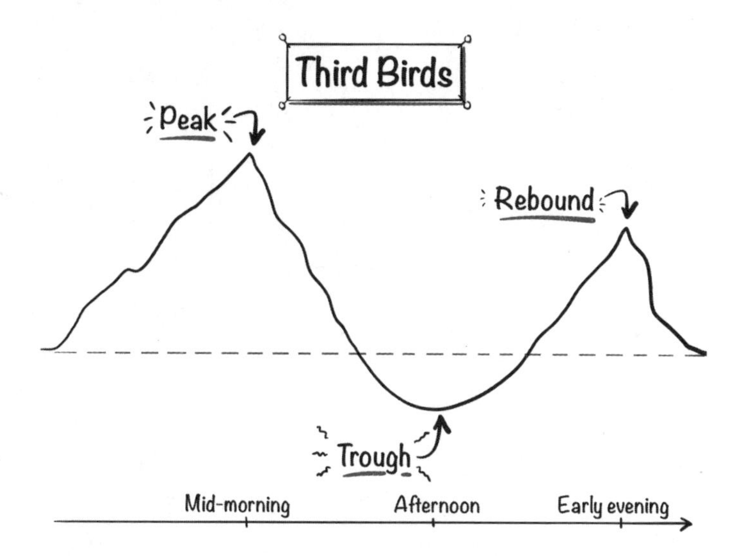

Owls, on the other hand, have a completely different experience. Their energy phases are rebound, trough, peak. They *begin* their day in rebound. That means they have *some* natural morning energy, but they're not as alert as a lark or third bird. But, just like larks and third birds, they're at their worst in the afternoon. Finally, they end the day with their energetic and alert peak in the late afternoon and evening.

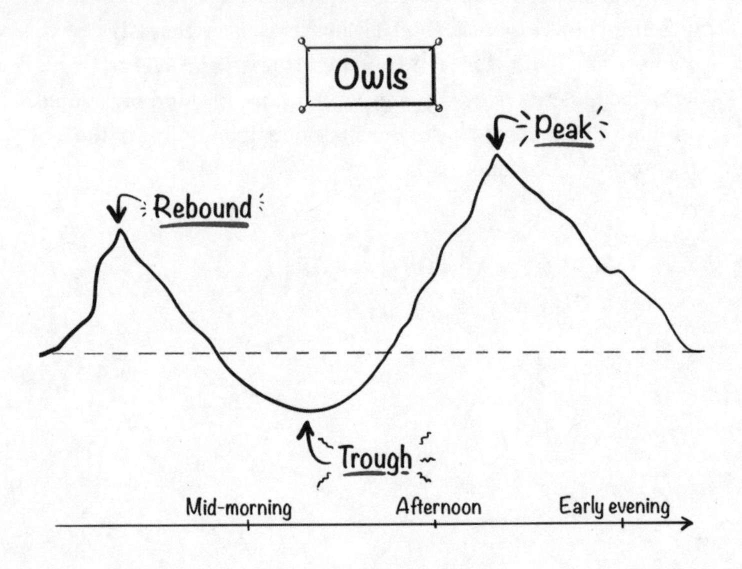

• • •

Now that you know which endeavors are the best fit for each of the three energy levels *and* you know your biological chronotype's unique energy pattern, you can pair the right work with the right energy level to maximize your productivity. As you move through your day armed with this insight, pay attention to how you feel at different times. When do you notice yourself beginning to feel sluggish? When do you transition from your trough to your rebound, or your peak time? The more in tune you become with your energy levels, the more strategic you can be about matching up the right work with the right time.

ENERGIZE YOUR TO-DO LIST

Just like all hours of the day are not created equal, all tasks are not created equal. In Part I you learned about the Pareto principle and that 80 percent of effects are created by 20 percent of causes. In your work, 20 percent of your work activities are responsible for 80 percent of your results. This also means that 20 percent of what's on your to-do list, or required for your job, is responsible for 80 percent of your success. Of course, that doesn't mean that the other 80 percent of your work is worthless, but it's definitely not pulling the same weight as the most impactful 20 percent.

If we know that 20 percent of what's on our to-do list gives us 80 percent of our results, it also means that the more time we can spend on those 20 percent tasks, the more successful we'll be. But how do we zero in on those 20 percent tasks when we have so many different responsibilities? Just like knowing your biological chronotype helps you identify your high energy hours in the day, scheduling your high energy work during your high energy hours can take your productivity to new levels.

Think about how you spent your time working last week. Every workweek has its ups and downs. There were likely moments that you begrudgingly trudged through tasks that had to be done, even though you didn't enjoy the work you were doing. Hopefully you can also picture yourself breezing through projects that didn't even feel like work because you were actually having fun. Chances are there were times you felt distracted and other times when you were so bored with your work you could barely stay focused.

Just like all hours in the day are not created equal, every item on our to-do list has the potential to energize us, completely drain us, or make us feel somewhere in between based on our level of passion and proficiency for each task.

Passion describes how much you enjoy the work you're doing. Having high passion for a task means you love doing it; low passion means you despise doing it.

Proficiency is how good you are at performing a certain task. High proficiency means you're great at doing it. Your proficiency could be natural, or perhaps you've cultivated your skills over time through education or practice. Low proficiency means you aren't very good at the task at all.

Hopefully, the activities you're passionate about and proficient at are the same and comprise the core of your job responsibilities.

Unfortunately, if we're not paying attention, it's possible to get caught up on the required tasks at hand and spend a lot of time on work we don't enjoy, and even on work we're not good at. Perhaps you've taken on tasks that aren't a good fit for you, either because you've said yes to too many things for fear of not seeming like a team player, or because the systems for automating or delegating the work aren't in place. Work like this lowers productivity, increases the likelihood of procrastination, and decreases overall happiness and satisfaction at work. Suddenly, you don't feel fulfilled in your job anymore. You feel completely drained and exhausted—and soon enough, you start looking for a way out.

The good news is that doesn't have to be your reality. And, you can change this by understanding the five different zones of work.

GETTING TO WHAT'S MOST IMPORTANT: YOUR GENUIS ZONE

All your tasks and to-dos can be organized into one of five different zones of work, and each zone is either an energy booster or an energy drainer. The first four zones—Genius Zone, Disinterest Zone,

Distraction Zone, and Drudgery Zone—form a grid based on the level of passion and proficiency you have for the tasks within each zone. The fifth zone, your Development Zone, doesn't fit neatly into the grid, but it is still a crucial part of it.

Just as all hours in the day are not created equal based on your energy levels, these five zones of work are not created equal. Your Genius Zone is by far the most important and the most impactful when it comes to how you spend your time.

Your goal will be to spend the most time working in your Genius Zone, which is work you're both passionate about and proficient at.

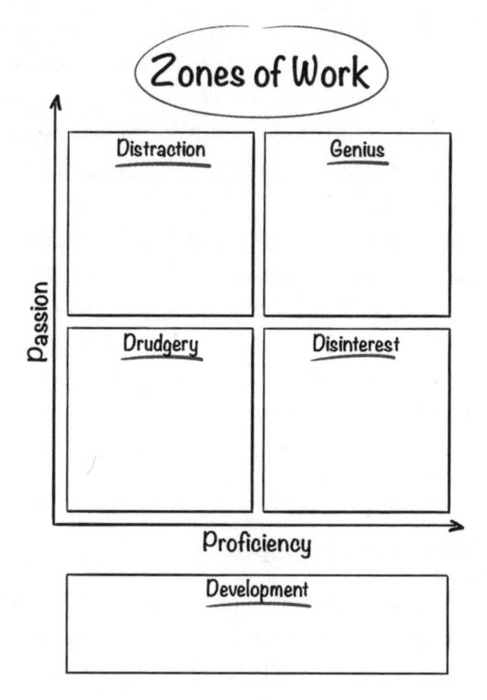

In the following three steps, inspired by authors Gay Hendricks and Michael Hyatt, we'll dive deeper into each of the five zones and categorize each of your activities so you will have more clarity than ever on how you are spending your time. And, you can start adjusting your calendar to allocate more time to spend on the highly skilled, energizing work that you love—while strategically offloading the rest to make the most of your limited time.

Let's work through those three steps.

Step 1: Make a List

To zero in on your energizing Genius Zone work, start by making a list of what you typically do each week. Grab recent to-do lists. Open your task management system. Look at your calendar. You can even grab your job description if you have one and the time study discussed in Chapter 4. The more detail we can add to your list, the more impactful this exercise will be for you.

One potential pitfall to watch out for: It can be tempting to leave low-impact tasks off the list because you know they're not how you should be spending your time. Even activities like organizing your email into folders, scanning receipts into your accounting software, and engaging in social media research by scrolling your newsfeed deserve to be included. Be as honest with yourself as possible and put it *all* on the list. This will give you the best results and a foundation for your next steps.

Step 2: Categorize Your List

Once you've compiled your list, you'll soon see that every single task and to-do fits into one of the five zones. But before organizing and categorizing, we need to understand each of the five zones.

As you know, your *Genius Zone* is work you love doing and you're great at. You are highly passionate about this work. It lights you up. You look forward to it and you're also highly proficient at these tasks. Whether you're naturally adept or you've spent years engaged in study or practice, you're very skilled at these tasks. With the unbeatable combination of high passion and high proficiency, it should come as no surprise that your Genius Zone houses your most energizing work. You're mostly likely to find yourself in a state of focus or flow when engaged in these tasks, and you'd spend all of your time working in your Genius Zone if you could.

Besides your Genius Zone, there are three "danger zones": the Drudgery Zone, Distraction Zone, and Disinterest Zone.

The *Drudgery Zone* is filled with the work you hate doing and are not good at. This low-passion, low-proficiency zone drains your energy, and it's usually the stuff on your to-do list that you procrastinate doing. This is a "danger zone" because your disdain for these activities makes it difficult for you to stay focused, and your tendency to give in to distraction can lead to mistakes and make this work take longer than it should.

Financial analysis and planning falls squarely in my Drudgery Zone. I don't enjoy running the numbers in my business, and I find a lot of the formulas and requirements to be confusing. Plus, I have no desire to improve my accounting skills. That's why I'm grateful to work with both a CPA and a financial coach who have business finance in their Genius Zones.

The *Distraction Zone* is where you categorize the work that you enjoy doing, but you're not actually good at. It's high passion, but low proficiency. Distraction Zone activities are energizing time wasters. Even though you're having fun, you're unable to make a significant contribution with this work. This is another danger zone because even though you're having fun, you're not accomplishing much. The time could be better spent in your Genius Zone.

My friend Diana, a wedding photographer, admits that updating her website is a Distraction Zone activity for her. She loves updating photo galleries, tweaking the page layouts, switching out colors, and creating graphics. Unfortunately, she is not very skilled at any of this, so her attempts at making changes often result in hours of wasted time fixing mistakes she's made. Plus, the changes she makes don't add value to her site. If Diana outsourced her website updates to someone with more proficiency, she could spend more time working in her Genius Zone—and creating more business for herself.

Social media research falls into the Distraction Zone for most, too. While time spent scrolling Facebook, Instagram, Twitter, or TikTok to gather inspiration for your marketing strategy can be helpful, set a limit for yourself. Get in, get out, get on with your day.

Your *Disinterest Zone* is often tricky, because you have a high proficiency in these tasks, but your passion is low. You're great at doing this stuff, but you just don't enjoy it. Because of your low passion for these tasks, they drain your energy.

Often, Disinterest Zone tasks stay on our to-do lists too long. We justify keeping them there because of our high skill level, which allows us to knock them out quickly when we get around to them—provided we get around to them. If you've ever procrastinated for weeks over a task that only took 15 minutes once you forced yourself to do it, you're likely dealing with a Disinterest Zone activity. This is a danger zone because it takes us away from more meaningful, energizing work that we actually enjoy.

The final zone, which doesn't fit neatly into the passion and proficiency grid, is the *Development Zone*. Development Zone activities are those you have *some* passion for but your proficiency isn't there . . . yet.

Perhaps you're a beginner who is kind of good at these tasks, and you think that you could love this work if you continued your study or improve your skills. Development Zone tasks are those that could someday be categorized in your Genius Zone.

For Kimberly, a former client, CPA, and certified tax coach, public speaking is one of her Development Zone activities. She'd always been curious about speaking and loved the idea of stepping on stage to tell her story and demystify money for mothers. So, she began working with a public speaking coach to improve her proficiency. By learning the key tenets of storytelling and speaking, mixed with lots of practice,

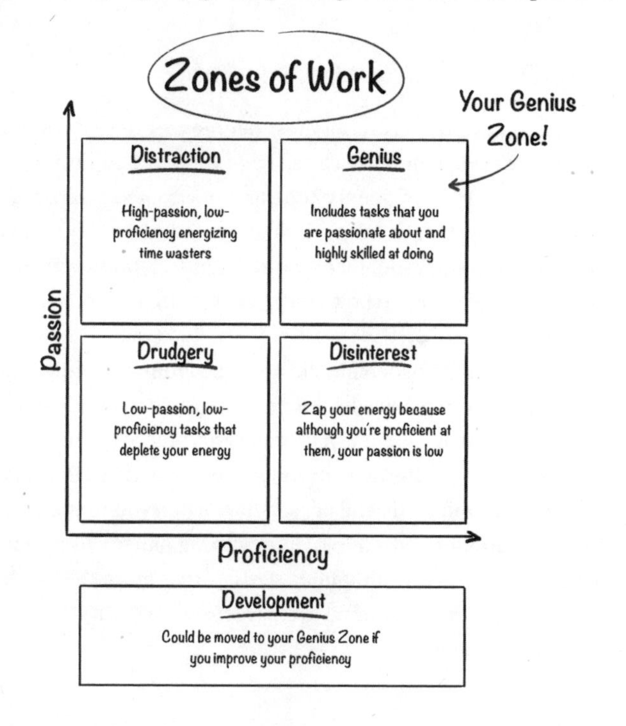

Kimberly is well on her way to making public speaking one of her Genius Zone activities.

• • •

Now that we understand the five zones, it's time to categorize your tasks and to-do items into their corresponding zone. I've found it helpful to draw a grid on a white board, a blank white sheet of paper, or a large wall-sized sticky note poster. Once you've created your grid, write each task in the appropriate zone based on your level of passion and proficiency for that task.

Step 3: Unload Your Danger Zones

At this point in our exercise, most people feel one of two ways. Either you're excited because you see that you're spending most of your time working in your Genius Zone and now you see the opportunity to pair your best, peak energy hours with your best, most energizing work to take your productivity to new heights. If that's you, awesome! Keep reading to find out how you can maximize your time and energy even more.

Or, you might be feeling the opposite. Your head might be spinning because you realize that you're not spending much time in your Genius Zone at all. Suddenly, it's clear why you're not happy at work, why you're not as effective or productive as you'd like to be, and why you feel worn out at the end of each day. When you're spending more time in your energy-draining, time-wasting danger zones than your Genius Zone, you feel unfulfilled. Plus, you're more easily exhausted because of the effort required to stay focused on tasks you're not good at and don't enjoy.

If you want to spend more time in your high-energy Genius Zone, you've got to unload your danger zones by doing one of three things: eliminate, automate, or delegate.

Eliminate

Review the tasks in your Disinterest, Drudgery, and Distraction Zones with a critical eye. What can you stop doing? What on your grid is simply a time waster that doesn't make a valuable impact in your day? I challenge you to cut 10 percent of the things on your grid, or to look for creative ways to replace or reduce time spent doing danger zone work. Even if you can't completely eliminate 10 percent, the process of thinking critically about what's truly worth your time is beneficial.

When one of my time management coaching clients, Nicole, looked closely at her Genius Zone grid and her time study log, she realized that she was spending a few hours each week driving to the post office to ship materials for training workshops she conducted across the country. This time in the car, often stuck in slow-moving traffic, was cutting into time she could be spending on impactful work or with her family. She eliminated this time waster by scheduling USPS package pickup once a week. By creatively replacing post office trips with package pickup, she was able to get back four to five hours each week to spend on more high-value tasks.

Automate

Once you've identified opportunities to eliminate things from your danger zones, review what's left. Of the remaining tasks, what can be automated? Is there anything you're currently doing manually that could be automated with a service, software, or template?

If you're spending time each week or month manually paying your bills, could you automate this process using auto draft or autopay features? Are you currently creating client invoices or proposals by creating documents, saving them as PDFs, and emailing them to clients to print, sign, scan, and return? Consider transitioning those administrative and financial processes to a client relationship management system (CRM) that can automate invoicing, facilitate e-signatures on digital contracts, and house templates for proposals. If scheduling appointments and managing your calendar is in your danger zone, try a scheduling tool like Calendly or Clockwise to remove yourself from the process.

In addition to automation tools, templates are another form of simplification through automation. Emails, invoices, proposals, reports, and contracts, anything you send more than once can be templatized. When do you find yourself saying the same thing over and over again? Instead of reinventing the wheel each time you answer the same frequently asked question, copy and paste the answer from a template and customize it for the specific situation.

Delegate

After you've identified what you can eliminate and automate, the remaining items in your danger zones likely need a human touch to be completed. We simply can't cut or automate everything. With what's left, what can you delegate to someone on your team? If you don't have a team, could you hire a contractor or an employee to handle any of these tasks?

One of my former time management coaching clients took bold action on her Genius Zone and worked with her supervisor to identify opportunities to delegate some of the danger zone work that had been added to her plate. Over time, the addition of this low-value work was eating away at the hours she should have been spending performing the core duties of her job. Identifying what was in her Genius Zone, and what wasn't, prepared her to have a frank conversation with her supervisor about responsibilities and time allocation. As a result, her organization created a position and hired a new team member. With less danger zone work, she was able to make more impactful progress on her projects, exceeding her goals and bringing massive success to her team.

THE RIGHT WORK AT THE RIGHT TIME

It's clear that all hours of the day are not created equal, and all tasks on our to-do lists are not created equal. But when you know which hours are the best for you, and you know which tasks make you feel excited and energized, you can create your own unique combination of the right work at the right time to become more productive and impactful with your work. We're certainly not robots, and we do have limits—but you can take your productivity to new heights when you know your biological chronotype and what's in your Genius Zone.

ESSENTIAL TAKEAWAYS

- Everyone experiences three energy phases each day: a high-energy peak, a low-energy trough, and a mid-level rebound. Your peak and rebound are ideal for focused work. Your trough is best used for low-impact work or taking a break.
- When you know your personal biological chronotype, you're able to create a schedule that syncs with the energy ebbs and flows of your day. You can plan better, be more productive, and use your energy to your advantage when making decisions about how to spend your time.
- Your tasks can be categorized into five zones of work based on your level of passion and proficiency. Your Genius Zone includes tasks you are passionate about and highly skilled at doing. Your Drudgery Zone is for low-passion, low-proficiency tasks that deplete your energy. Distraction Zone tasks are high-passion, low-proficiency energizing time wasters. Disinterest Zone tasks zap your energy because although you're proficient at them, your passion is low. Your Development Zone is for activities that could be moved to your Genius Zone if you improve your proficiency.
- When you have a clear understanding of what's in your high-energy Genius Zone, you can offload your energy-draining tasks by eliminating, automating, and delegating. Then, you're equipped to create a more strategic schedule that pairs your energy-giving work with your high-energy times of day for maximum productivity.

Get Focused

Multitasking is a lie. There, I said it.

I hate to be the bearer of bad news, but multitasking just isn't real. You might be great at staying on top of multiple projects concurrently in motion, but you scientifically cannot focus on more than one thing at a time. So, if you've ever told a coworker, boasted in a job interview, or noted on a résumé that you're great at multitasking, you unintentionally told a fib.

THE TRUTH ABOUT MULTITASKING

Researchers at the University of Utah have found that people don't multitask because they're good at doing two things at once. Instead, they jump from task to task because they can't control the urge to give in to distraction. "They have trouble inhibiting the impulse to do another activity," explained psychology professor David Sanbonmatsu.[1]

What does that mean? People don't multitask because they're *good* at multitasking. They multitask because they're *bad* at focusing.

At the beginning of every episode of *It's About Time*, my podcast about work, life, and balance, I remind listeners that "around here, busy is *not* a badge of honor." Similarly, being "good" at multitasking is absolutely *not* a badge of honor.

When you're doing multiple things at once like checking social media, writing a proposal, and replying to text messages, it might *feel* like you're multitasking. But, what you're actually doing is context switching.

Context switching, as discussed in earlier chapters, is switching your focus between unrelated tasks. It *feels* productive, even though context switching actually increases mistakes.[2] Unfortunately, our brains *love* it. Skipping from task to task creates a dopamine-addiction feedback loop that rewards your brain for losing focus and searching for some kind of new external stimulation. You read that right. It's almost as if our brains don't *want* us to focus, which is why it takes so much effort to stick to one task at a time.

According to computer scientist and psychologist Gerald Weinberg, taking on additional tasks simultaneously can destroy up to 80 percent of your productive time.[3] You can't manage your time well or do your best work when your attention is scattered across 12 open apps, 34 ongoing conversations, and a to-do list a mile long. We absolutely must focus in order to get real work done. Knowing what's in your Genius Zone, as you learned in Chapter 9, won't be as impactful if you're not able to *stay* in your Genius Zone for longer than three minutes at a time.

Armed with the fresh knowledge that multitasking isn't real, now we can embark on our journey to fewer distractions and deeper focus.

In this chapter, we spotlight three strategies you can start using today to cut back on context switching. Then, we'll strengthen our focus muscle with three mental workouts.

THREE STRATEGIES FOR SUPER FOCUS

While there are a multitude of focus hacks and productivity methods that can improve focus, we'll look at three. First, we'll look for opportunities to set clear expectations with those around us. Then, we'll create an environment for focus. Finally, we'll use a timer to stay focused for longer stretches of time.

Super Focus Strategy 1: Set Expectations

Whether you work from home with kids nearby, do your job in an open concept workspace, or take meetings in your private office, focusing your attention takes a village. Setting expectations with those around you and letting them know that you need focused time will remove some of potential distractions that might come your way during that time. When you know you'll need uninterrupted time to focus, plan ahead and communicate that need to others. Use your Ideal Week and your Weekly Planning Session to identify those critical focus hours in advance. Remember, no one can read our minds and sometimes we have to ask for exactly what we need in order to get it.

Communicating your need for focus time can be done in several ways. The most obvious opportunity is to verbally communicate that need. If you meet with your team on a regular basis, use this time as an opportunity for everyone to share when each needs time to focus in the week ahead. If your team uses Slack or another messaging system, make sure your status is accurate and communicates when you're available to chat and when you're focused on work. In a past open office setting, our team had signs we could put on our desks to signal we were engaged in deep focus. There are a number of ways that you can communicate your expectations in order to limit distractions, so try different methods to determine what works best with your team.

If you're afraid or feeling hesitant about setting expectations because you want to be available, consider the alternative. How long would this work take you *without* uninterrupted focus time? How will that delay affect those around you? Will it force you to work longer hours and affect your ability to be present with your family? Will it impact the timeline of your project and therefore put your team in a tough situation? When you consider the negative consequences of interruptions compared to the discomfort of setting expectations, taking a moment to ask for focus time might not be so bad after all.

Super Focus Strategy 2: Create an Environment for Focus

In *The Happiness Project,* author Gretchen Rubin shared her "Secrets of Adulthood," a list of principles she's compiled across her years as an adult. Her list of secrets contains maxims like, "Well begun is half done" and "Practice makes permanent." One of my favorites from her list applies to focus: "Outer order contributes to inner calm."

When you look around your workspace, every single piece of paper, unopened envelope, magazine, sticky note, and pile of materials represents a decision that needs to be made. Six hours of uninterrupted time can be completely derailed by a distracting environment. Instead of focusing on the work that *needs* to be done, you feel antsy surrounded by clutter that needs to be dealt with and decisions that need to be made. So, how can your environment work for you and not against you? A few ideas follow.

Be Consistent

When you consistently work in the same location, being in that location becomes a habit trigger. Your mind begins to equate being in that location with getting work done. Similar to a startup routine, working in a consistent environment creates a mindset shift that increases your ability to maintain focus on your most important work. I'm certainly not suggesting you never change locations or avoid working in a coffee shop or coworking space, but the more consistent your work environment, the more consistent your ability to focus.

Declutter Your Workspace

To set yourself up for focus success, challenge yourself to declutter your workspace at some point in the coming week. In fact, right now add a time block to your calendar dedicated to cleaning up and clearing out.

If your workspace is so cluttered it requires more than one time block to clean up, add multiple 30-minute time blocks to your calendar to tackle specific areas you need to clean. Then, at each scheduled time, set a timer and declutter as much as possible until the timer runs out. By decluttering one section at a time, your progress will be more obvious, and you'll build momentum to continue working your way through the space.

Set Up a Clutter-Free System

Once you've got the clutter under control in your workspace, create a system for managing incoming items (and potential clutter) moving forward. Consider adding an inbox tray to your desk to gather pieces of mail, magazines, and piles of stuff that makes its way into your space. If you don't have an inbox tray, repurpose something like a basket or a box and make it work. Then, make sure that emptying the inbox is part of your administrative task batch, and that the task batch has a home in your Ideal Week. Whether you add an inbox tray to your desk or you corral clutter into purposeful baskets or bins, maintaining a decluttered workspace reduces your decision fatigue and enables you to focus your attention on your work instead of the piles of stuff.

Out of Sight, Out of Mind

If your current workspace is a kitchen table rather than a corner office, do your best to position yourself with your back to distractions like dishes in the sink, the laundry piled on the sofa, or the TV silently begging you to turn on Netflix.

One of my time management coaching clients has a gorgeous home office with double French doors that face her living room. Although the light that pours in through the doors' glass panes is beautiful, the distractions caused by her toddlers banging on the glass while she tries to work is less than ideal. Since they can see her, they want to be with her while she works. Adding simple window shades to her French doors could work wonders to keep her focused and out of sight from her kids while they're with their nanny.

Audit Your Notifications

When's the last time you put down this book to check your phone? Chances are it was at least in the last 30 minutes.

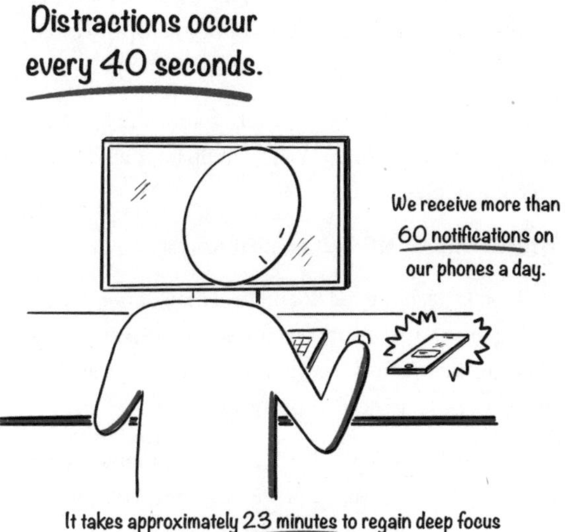

The average person is hit with a distraction every 40 seconds when working on a computer.[4] To make matters worse, smartphones beep, buzz, vibrate, and ding with more than 60 notifications on average per day.[5] When you factor in the approximately 23 minutes it takes to regain deep focus every time you're interrupted, it's a wonder we can get *anything* accomplished.[6] So even if your workspace is sparkling clean and clear of clutter, there's still work to be done to create an environment for focus.

To wrangle your digital clutter, do a notifications audit. Open up the notification settings on your smartphone. Right now. Go ahead and take a look at all of the different notifications that come your way on a daily basis and then ask yourself:

- Which of these notifications are necessary and actually make my life better? Calendar alerts, phone calls, and most *but not all* text messages are great examples of a helpful notification.
- Which notifications do I typically ignore and habitually swipe away when they pop up? What would happen if I turned them off completely?
- Which notifications bother me the most or make me uneasy?
- Do I really *need* the red dot on my email or messaging app telling me how many unread messages are waiting for me? Do I feel antsy when I see an unread message, even though I know it's probably not important?
- Where can I be selective with my notifications or customize them if I'm not comfortable turning them completely off?
- Can I adjust settings to change the type of alert I receive? For example, instead of getting a text box that pops up every time I get a Slack message, can I set it so I only see a red dot?

When you review your notifications, you're actually reviewing a list of distractions you have chosen to accept. Remember, you are in charge of your smartphone, and you are in control of when you are distracted or interrupted by it. You tell your phone what to do, not the other way around. When you think critically about the notifications you allow, and then consider what they interrupt, you can decide what's more important: the interruption or your focus. The alternative is to leave all of your notifications in the default setting and give your phone permission to boss you around.

Personally, I don't receive any kind of pop-up alert for text messages. Instead, I only know that I've received a text message when I look at my phone and see a red dot on the messages app. That's it. I decide when I see text messages, and I decide when I respond. My personal philosophy is that text messages don't require an immediate response. Anyone who is close enough to me to text me understands that I'll respond at the best time for me. Anyone who needs to communicate something to me urgently, like my family or children's school, knows to call.

Once you've completed your notifications audit and streamlined your smartphone settings, do the same for your computer, tablet, and any other devices that have their own notification settings. Remember, your devices exist for *your* convenience, not the convenience of everyone who wants to interrupt you throughout the day.

Clear Your Desktop and Downloads

A cluttered and overwhelming computer desktop, downloads folder, and digital filing system is the equivalent of your physical workspace being covered in random, unrelated papers. Knowledge workers (aka anyone who spends most of their time behind a laptop) spend almost 20 percent of their time searching for information.[7] That's a little more than an hour and a half of an eight-hour day!

To cut your search time and spend more time on what matters, set a recurring weekly reminder to clear your desktop and move files to the appropriate locations, even if that location is the trash. Do the same with your downloads folder. For many, the downloads folder becomes a bottomless pit of files that are downloaded and then never moved to their proper place. Finally, if you use a shared file storage system like Google Drive or OneDrive, set aside time once a week, month, or quarter to do a sweep of your files and folders. Move any stray files to their correct folders, delete or archive unneeded files, and make sure your current organization and file naming system is still serving you.

Super Focus Strategy 3: Use the Pomodoro Method

Named for Italian business student Francesco Cirillo's tomato-shaped kitchen timer, the Pomodoro method is a time management technique that can supercharge your productivity during your workday.

In the late 1980s, Cirillo was experimenting with different methods for increasing his concentration while studying. Using a kitchen timer, he segmented his work into intervals with short breaks in between. After four rounds, he'd take a longer break. After experimenting with different durations of work and rest times, he discovered that 25-minute work intervals with 5-minute breaks were his sweet spot for focus without fatigue. Since his kitchen timer was shaped like a tomato, and the Italian word for *tomato* is *pomodoro*, the Pomodoro method was born.

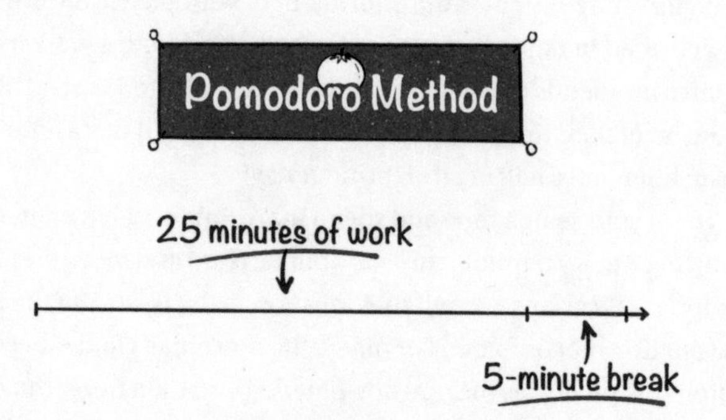

Using the Pomodoro method for focus is ideal for working your way through complex projects across a few hours because it helps with focusing on a single task and decreases context switching. Also, when you know that you have a five-minute break approaching, you're able to stay motivated because you know there's an end in sight. Setting mini-goals for your 25-minute work intervals gives you the opportunity to celebrate small wins along the way, too.[8] Plus, taking small breaks means you feel less tired at the end of the day.

Here's how to use the Pomodoro method to stay focused in seven simple steps:

1. Decide what you're going to work on. Remember, the goal is to focus on only one task for a long period of time.
2. Get a timer. You can use a kitchen timer, your smartphone timer, or an app specifically designed for the Pomodoro method. Pomofocus.io has been my go-to while writing this book.
3. Set your timer for 25 minutes and focus on your chosen task until the timer beeps.
4. Set your timer for five minutes and take a break.
5. Repeat 25-minute work intervals followed by 5-minute breaks three more times.
6. After four 25-minute work periods, take a longer break for 15–30 minutes.
7. Repeat as needed.

To get the most out of the Pomodoro method, make sure that your Ideal Week includes a few time blocks dedicated to using this method for focused work.

It's even better if you're able to schedule your focus time to align with your peak energy hours. Set expectations with others when you're planning a round of Pomodoros and create an environment for focus by doing a quick declutter before you begin working. Finally, keep a notepad nearby to corral self-interruptions and stray thoughts.

When you use these three techniques for focus, whether alone or in combination, you'll be shocked at how much progress you'll make on your most important work.

NOW IT'S TIME TO FLEX YOUR FOCUS MUSCLE

While setting expectations, clearing your environment from distractions, and using the Pomodoro method can help you stay focused in the short term, increasing your capacity for focus is a long game. Chances are your mind wanders much more than you realize. A Harvard study found that we spend 47 percent of our waking hours daydreaming—meaning we spend *eight hours* of our time awake not paying attention to what's happening right in front of us.[9]

While this might sound like a hopeless situation for our ability to pay attention, the good news is that it's possible to improve your focus. Just like the training montage in the 1976 movie *Rocky*, you can practice, put in the reps, and actually increase your attention span. Consider me your personal trainer with these three exercises to flex your focus muscle.

Focus Muscle Exercise 1: Monotask

To kick off our workout, we're starting small. Here's your assignment: do just one thing. Instead of multitasking, monotask. If you're raising your eyebrows because this exercise sounds too simple to be effective, give it a try. Doing just one thing is easier said than done.

Remember, we get distracted every 40 seconds. Our brains desperately want to switch tasks because it gives us a dopamine boost that makes us *feel* productive, even when we're not.

To begin monotasking, start small. Very small. Grab a timer. A simple kitchen timer is best. Using your smartphone or laptop as a timer will tempt you to compulsively pop over to other apps. Set your timer for 10 minutes and then do just one thing for those 10 minutes. Anytime you feel your mind begin to wander, go back to your original task. If something pops into your mind that you don't want to forget, jot it down on a notepad and get back to work.

Research shows that when you repeatedly make a conscious effort to refocus on your work after your mind wanders, over time, you heighten your executive control—the thinking and planning part of your brain that lives in your prefrontal cortex. Every time you refocus, you reinforce the habit, which gradually becomes stronger over time.

After a few rounds of monotasking practice for 10 minutes at a time, consider upping your timer to 15 minutes and work your way up to 25-minute Pomodoros.

Focus Muscle Exercise 2: Have a Mindful Mealtime

When's the last time you ate a meal alone without glancing at your phone, watching TV, or reading something on the internet to pass the time as you ate? If it's been a while, you're not alone. One-third of Americans can't get through an entire meal without looking at their phones.[10]

Mindfulness is the practice of doing one thing deliberately. It's monotasking. Next time you sit down to eat lunch, instead of checking your phone or catching up on a show, monotask your meal. Set a timer

for 5–10 minutes. Then, eat your lunch and focus on each bite. Focus on the flavors. Feel the textures of the food, your fork, and your drink. Anytime you feel your mind begin to wander, direct your focus back to eating. If monotasking during lunch feels daunting, start with a snack. This is mindful eating.

During your monotasked meal, you'll likely be surprised by two things. First, how frequently your mind wanders. Second, how delicious food can be when you slow down enough to really enjoy it.

You can do the same thing with any activity, from folding laundry or washing dishes to brushing your teeth or vacuuming your living room. Focus on just that activity and bring yourself back to the task at hand whenever you feel your mind begin to wander. Every time you refocus, you're doing another rep to strengthen your attention.

Focus Muscle Exercise 3: Meditate

Mindfulness and meditation are two sides of the same coin. Mindfulness is something you practice as you do something else (like the mindful meal in our previous exercise). Meditation, however, is done by itself. Both mindfulness and meditation have the same amazing benefits.

There are a multitude of meditation resources online and in books, but here's a super simple step-by-step guide to meditation to get you started:

1. Find somewhere you won't be distracted. Set expectations with others around you if you need to.

2. Sit upright in a chair, on the floor—wherever. You should feel relaxed, but alert. Sit up straight but don't be overly rigid.

3. Close your eyes (or don't). Whatever helps you feel more alert and focused.

4. Set a timer or use a meditation app like Headspace or Calm. Start with five minutes and see how it feels.

5. Once you start your timer, focus on your breath. Don't try to control it or analyze it, just notice it.

6. Whenever your mind begins to wander, and it most definitely will, bring your attention back to your breath. And repeat. Whenever your mind wanders, don't judge or be hard on yourself, just acknowledge it and go back to your breath.

• • •

Strengthening your attention muscle is a long game. It takes practice and consistency. Over time, tools like monotasking, mindfulness, and meditation will enable you to focus on your work better than ever before. Bringing your best focus to your most important work and doing that work at the right time for you is a recipe for next level time management and the ability to create more space for spending time on what matters most to you.

ESSENTIAL TAKEAWAYS

- When we think we're multitasking, we're actually context switching. Context switching destroys our productivity and weakens our focus.
- Setting expectations with others about our need for uninterrupted focus time, creating both a physical and digital environment for focus, and using the Pomodoro method can improve your focus, impacting your productivity and ability to manage your time.
- Although we spend 47 percent of our waking hours daydreaming, it is possible to improve your ability to focus for longer periods of time by practicing monotasking, mindfulness, and meditation.

Get Rest

Have you heard of a "limiting belief"? Until I began studying to become a coach, I'd never heard those two words used together. Now, I help my clients blast through their limiting beliefs in order to unlock more Purpose, productivity, and intention in their lives on a regular basis.

A limiting belief is a thought that holds you back from doing something. It's believing that an *opinion* is actually fact and then allowing that opinion to keep you from moving forward or growing. Basically, it's something you believe that causes you to stay stuck.

One of the limiting beliefs that I've struggled with throughout my life is this: I'm not good at resting.

I recognize how ridiculous that might sound, but I'll bet that there are some self-described high achievers, go-getters, or Type A readers nodding their heads in silent agreement, maybe even cringing a little because they've felt the same way at some point.

I'm not good at resting. How can one be bad at resting? There's no competition for "best rester." No one is grading our naps or tallying the minutes we spend on break during our workdays. "I'm not good at resting" is a lie; one I told myself for far too long.

In the past, I've used this lie as an excuse to go, go, go. To never stop moving, and always find just one more thing to do. Since I'm not good at resting, I might as well keep doing. Bedtime? What's that? Five-minute breaks while using the Pomodoro method? I'd skip them and keep working. A late-night request from a crisis communications client? I'm on it.

It's no wonder that after a decade of always *doing* and rarely resting I finally had enough. I learned the hard way that rest is far too important to put on the back burner, shrug off, or skip. We genuinely can't afford to believe that we're not good at rest. Our health, and therefore our lives depend on it. If your health isn't enough to spark your curiosity about how to become a better rester, your performance at work, creativity, and progress toward your biggest goals are all counting on you to make time for rest, too.

THE MOST UNDERRATED TIME MANAGEMENT STRATEGY

Rest does *not* get the credit it deserves for being a key ingredient in becoming the best version of ourselves. Imagine sitting in a job interview or talking with a news reporter and being asked, "So tell me about some of your strengths," and responding with, "Well, I'm really great at resting. In fact, I consider rest to be just as important as hard work." In most cases, it's likely you'd be met with a scrunched face and furrowed eyebrows.

As a culture, rest has been looked down upon and the need for rest considered a weakness by many. You don't have to scroll very far on LinkedIn to find another post from an entrepreneur touting "hustle" as the secret to their success. You'll see them sharing their philosophies of work in the form of short, pithy statements shouting things like *Put in the work! Hustle till you drop! Don't stop, just hustle!*

After repeatedly absorbing messages like this—whether posted on social media, printed on coffee mugs, or plastered on office decor—you might even begin to believe that rest is for the weak, and if you're not always working, then you're not working enough.

What the "hustlers" usually leave out of their glorification of busy are the unglamorous photos of battling exhaustion, the relationships that have disintegrated due to neglect, and the toll their workaholic tendencies have taken on their health.

What I've found is that *rest* is the most underrated time management strategy, and the most underrated strategy for success. Getting enough rest impacts your health, creativity, and focus, as well as your ability to avoid burnout. Without rest, your health is in jeopardy. If you're not healthy, none of the tips and strategies in this book matter.

In addition to being overlooked as a key aspect of our professional health, we tend to only think of rest as sleep. Of course, sleep is essential, but there's more to rest than the seven to nine hours of shut-eye you need each night.

In this chapter, we'll remind ourselves why rest is nonnegotiable. Then, we'll look at three ways to incorporate intentional rest into our lives. From creating a ritual for a restful night's sleep and taking breaks throughout your workday to designating slower seasons throughout the year, you'll be equipped with a well-rounded arsenal of recharge ideas that will have you confidently believing you *are* good at resting.

GET ENOUGH SLEEP

Anyone who's worked late into the night, pulled an all-nighter, experienced transcontinental jet lag, or been the parent to young children can attest to the negative impacts of missing a few hours of sleep.

Despite being exhausted, it's common for many adults to refuse an earlier bedtime. After neglecting to schedule any time for themselves as they race around meeting work deadlines and caring for their families without a break, many find their only "free" time comes at night. Since people don't want to lose that late-night time for themselves, sleep gets shortchanged. So continues the cycle of exhaustion: very little time for themselves, staying up late . . . repeat.

Sometimes after an exceptionally tiring week, we tell ourselves we'll catch up on sleep over the weekend. Unfortunately, that's not an effective strategy. For every hour of lost sleep, it takes four days to fully recover—*four days*.

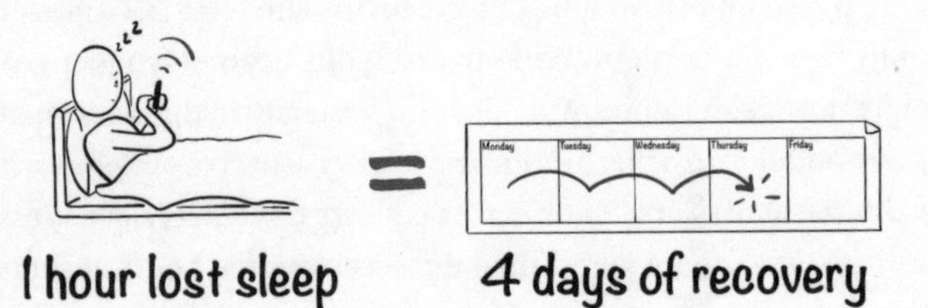

Missing out on those essential seven to nine hours of shut-eye has effects far beyond feeling a little sleepy during a morning meeting. Not getting enough sleep negatively affects your short-term and long-term memory. It impacts your concentration, problem-solving ability, and creativity. Drowsy driving increases your risk for car accidents and injury. Missing sleep weakens your immune system, lowers your sex drive, and affects your balance and coordination.

Needless to say, if you want to be successful during the day, you absolutely must prioritize getting good sleep at night.

Four Strategies for Better Sleep

To give good sleep the time in your schedule it deserves, try the following four strategies.

Sleep Strategy 1: Create a Cozy Environment for Sleep

Just like we intentionally created an environment for focus in Chapter 10, it's helpful to create an environment that supports sound sleep, too. Start by blocking out light with blackout curtains or shades, or consider using a sleep mask. Excess light exposure, even from a tiny light in your bedroom, can impact your circadian rhythm and melatonin production.

Keep your room cool. The best temperature for sleep is between 60°–67°F. If your room gets too hot or too cold, you're more likely to wake up. Your core body temperature drops a bit as a part of the process of falling asleep, so a too hot room can keep you awake. Keep a fan in your room to regulate the temperature, and consider swapping out bedsheets and blankets based on the season.

Create *your* version of peace and quiet. Some people sleep best with complete silence, others prefer white noise. White noise apps and sound machines can hide house noises, unwanted nature sounds, or the rumble of traffic outside. If you're currently trying to sleep in silence, but your racing mind is keeping you awake at night, consider trying a white noise app. The staticky sound of white noise can give your mind something to focus on as you're falling asleep instead of ruminating on your to-do list.

Keep paper and a pen beside your bed if you deal with this, too. If your mind is racing and you can't sleep, pull out a notebook and start writing. If you have an idea and you don't want to forget it before morning, jot it down. If you've got worries, write them down. When thoughts are bouncing around as you're trying to fall asleep, get them out of your head and on paper. Then turn off the light and go to sleep.

Sleep Strategy 2: Choose a Consistent Wakeup Time Each Day

For the longest time, I thought bedtime had the biggest impact on your ability to get a good night's sleep. However, it turns out that your circadian rhythm is guided by the time you wake up! When you wake up at a consistent time each morning, you're establishing a pattern for your internal clock to follow. This pattern triggers your body to fall asleep easily at a predictable time each evening, setting you up for rested success the next day.

Choose a wakeup time and stick with it, even on the weekends. This will train your body to keep a healthy and consistent sleep schedule. After you choose your wakeup time, set your sleep budget. Count seven to nine hours backward from your wakeup time and prioritize being asleep by that time.

Sleep Strategy 3: Design a Sleep-Oriented Nighttime Ritual

While an evening routine is typically designed to help us prepare to end the day, incorporating intentional sleep-supporting activities in your routine can improve your likelihood of a solid night's sleep. Start winding down at least 30 minutes before you plan to turn off the lights.

If you're using bright overhead lighting, switch over to a lamp or use a dimmer switch.

Whether you like to soak in the bathtub, take a hot shower, or have an eight-step skin care routine, perform your nighttime sleep ritual in the same order every night. This signals your mind and body that it's time to wind down for sleep.

Most importantly, set a reminder to turn off your screens at least 30 minutes before bedtime, even better if you can shut them off two hours before. Too much screen time in the evening can disrupt your natural melatonin production that guides your circadian rhythm.

Start Getting Ready for Sleep Long Before Bedtime

Even with a bedtime ritual in place, preparing for a good night's sleep begins much earlier in the day. Aim to get some exercise each day, even if it's just a walk outside. Moving your body during the day promotes good sleep at night. However, make sure your workout is at least two to three hours before bedtime. Working out can make you feel too energized or stimulated to sleep, and the increase in your body temperature can impact your ability to fall asleep.

Avoid eating too late. Just like it's recommended to cut off exercise several hours before bed, finish your last big meal of the day prior to that two- to three-hour window. This allows some time for digestion and reduces your chances of getting heartburn.

Finally, watch your caffeine intake. If you find yourself wide awake at night, think back to what time you had your last caffeinated beverage. Experiment with cutting off caffeine at different times of the day and pay attention to how you feel at night. After trial and error, I've learned that my afternoon iced coffee must be finished no later than 2:45 p.m. if I want to sleep well.

TAKE A BREAK

While you sleep, your brain is in restoration mode. It's sorting and processing information from the day and creating new pathways to prepare you for tomorrow. It's also in healing mode, repairing blood vessels, producing collagen to repair your skin, and doing a whole host of other night shift reparative duties. But nighttime isn't the only time for restoration. Opportunities for restorative breaks that keep us happy, productive, and energized can happen throughout the day. Unfortunately, most of us don't take enough breaks, and our work and health suffers as a result.

When we take breaks, we make better decisions. We have more creative ideas and innovative solutions, and we can stay focused for longer periods of time. Without breaks, we start to suffer from decision fatigue, lack of focus, and damaged eyes from staring at screens. Taking breaks also strengthens our short-term and associative memory. (Your associative memory helps you put a face with a name. I know we could all use help remembering names from time to time.)

The best way to make breaks a regular part of your day is to plan them in advance and make them a regular part of your schedule. Your Ideal Week from Chapter 6 can include placeholders for short breaks throughout the day. As you bring more intention to your breaks during the day, keep the following best practices in mind.

Something Is Better Than Nothing

If we stay focused on a single task for too long, it's possible to lose sight of what we're trying to achieve. Taking frequent short breaks, like the five-minute breaks in the Pomodoro method, help maintain focus and reactivate commitment to a goal. A short break, even one to three minutes, can remind yourself what you're working toward so you can step out of the weeds for a moment. And if your time is limited, staring into space to rest your eyes for 20 seconds is better than nothing at all.

Moving Is Better Than Being Still

Walking around for a few minutes can increase energy levels, sharpen focus, boost mood, and reduce feelings of fatigue during a late afternoon trough. Taking a few minutes for these short bursts of energy can be more effective than a single 30-minute walk because they break up long periods of concentration.

A former colleague keeps a recurring appointment on his calendar dedicated to taking a walk each afternoon. Even if it's raining, he gets up from his desk and walks around his apartment to stretch his legs and feel a burst of natural energy. Whether you go for a daily walk, do some desk yoga, or get in a few kettlebell swings, setting aside some break time to move your body will boost your energy and your productivity.

Outside Is Better Than Inside

Taking a break outside in the fresh air is one of the most effective ways to take a restorative break. People who take short walks outside return with better moods than people who walk indoors. If you're stuck inside, even looking out the window or being near indoor plants can be restorative.

Years ago, I reported to a government building that I called "the cave." My office and the hallways on my floor had no windows. To see any sunshine during my workday, I had to take the elevator from the tenth to the first floor. To bring in some nature, I purchased a small plant for my office that I named Robert. He was as helpful as he could be in bringing some of the outside in, but there was no substitute for the mood boost that came from a walk in the sunshine.

During at least one break each day, aim to get outside. Take a walk around the block, or sit on a bench and read a book. Sometimes during hot Louisiana summers, I'll pour a glass of ice water and stand outside for a few minutes before I sweat into a puddle on the sidewalk. If it's storming outside or your office has no windows, look at some indoor plants. Anything green and living can be restorative.

With Someone Is Better Than Alone

If you have a preference for introversion, alone time can definitely be rejuvenating. However, research on restorative breaks points to the benefit of spending time with others, especially when we can choose the person. Sharing a break with someone else reduces stress, physical strain, and job turnover.[1]

At least once a week, take a break by calling a friend to catch up or write a handwritten note or card. Schedule a regular walking break with colleagues you like. If you work from home, occasionally make one of your Zoom meetings a walk and talk. Instead of sitting in front of your screen, grab your phone and have a good old-fashioned phone call to catch up while you take a walk around the block. If going on an afternoon coffee run is a part of your routine, invite a friend to join you, or drop off a treat to them on the way back to your desk.

No Work Is Better Than Some Work

Concentration is tough, that's why it's often the most valued and most important work we do. Taking a break helps you clear the mental cobwebs and make subconscious connections that help with problem solving. Allowing your mind to wander fosters creativity and innovation. Try meditation, controlled breathing, and even watching funny videos to give yourself a mental break.

That being said, try your best to go tech-free when possible. All too often, we take a break from our work by checking social media or responding to emails. However, when your break still includes work or tech, it doesn't register as a restorative break to your brain. It registers as more work, so you don't get the true benefit of taking the break. A break that's multitasked with work is wasted time. You don't step back into your work any more refreshed than when you stepped out. For full restorative benefits, challenge yourself to take a true tech-free, work-free break.

PLAN SEASONS OF REST

Taking breaks during your workday keeps your energy up so you can stay focused and productive. Taking a vacation, a *real* vacation where you don't do work, can replenish your motivation to continue working toward your goals. However, rest doesn't have to look like not working at all, and it can last much longer than your typical vacation. It's called a *season* of rest.

A season of rest looks like planning your work to include periods of intentional slowness, instead of trying to maintain a fast-paced tempo throughout the year.

Consider this. Football season is not year-round. The players take breaks for rest and for training, and then go hard once the season kicks off. Baseball and basketball seasons are the same. Even the Olympics are only every four years.

The on-season is a period of intense work, and giving it all you've got. The off-season is for resting, repairing, training, and preparing for the next season.

Based on your industry, there are times of year that naturally lend themselves to being busier, and some that are slower. In addition to industry factors, your geography may impact your busy and slower seasons. For example, Realtors typically experience a slower season during colder months. Colder, often dreary weather means fewer houses are on the market, and the busy holiday season is a less than ideal time for a move. Then, as the weather gets warmer the market heats up again. More homeowners decide to list, and more buyers are interested in seeing what's available. Realtors can use their slower season to rest, and to refine their systems and processes in preparation for the busier, warmer months.

REST

When considering all three of these types of rest—getting enough sleep, taking breaks, and planning for seasons of rest—it is not a multiple-choice question where you pick only one. All three need to be a regular part of your life.

You can get nine hours of sleep each night, but if you don't take breaks while you work, your creativity and your focus will suffer. If you take plenty of breaks throughout the day, but your year as a whole is nonstop, barreling from one major project to the next without breathing room, you're heading for burnout. And you can strategically plan your year so that periods of intense work are followed by rest, but if you're only getting five hours of sleep each night, your health will suffer.

Sleep, breaks, and seasons of rest work together to help you show up as your best self. Your best, rested self.

ESSENTIAL TAKEAWAYS

- Rest is one of the most important, yet underrated strategies for time management. Without proper rest and intentional recharge, other time management and productivity strategies are less effective.
- To give good sleep the time in your schedule it deserves, create an environment for sleep—choose a consistent waking time, design a bedtime ritual, and make choices during your day that set you up for sleep success.
- The best way to make breaks a regular part of your day is to plan them in advance. Take a walk, get outside, spend time with a friend, and do your best to avoid work and technology during your breaks in order to get the full restorative benefits.
- Rest doesn't have to look like not working at all. Instead of working at the same tempo all year, planning your year with intentional seasons of rest can help you maintain a predictable rhythm and healthy pace.

Notes

Chapter 3

1. Steel, P. *The Procrastination Equation: How to Stop Putting Things Off and Start Getting Stuff Done*. New York: HarperCollins Publishers, 2011.

Chapter 4

1. Mark, G., D. Gudith, & U. Klocke. (2008) "The Cost of Interrupted Work: More Speed and Stress," *CHI '08: Proceedings of the SIGCHI Conference on Human Factors in Computing Systems*, 107–110. https://dl.acm.org/doi/10.1145/1357054.1357072.

Chapter 8

1. "Fruitless Searching, Irrelevant Information, Inefficient Tools Contribute to Great Resignation." Coveo, Coveo Solutions, Inc., March 29, 2022. https://www.coveo.com/en/company/news-releases/2022/fruitless-searching-irrelevant-information-inefficient-tools-contribute-to-great-resignation.
2. Craig, A. "Discovery of 'Thought Worms' Opens Window to the Mind." Web log. *Queen's University* (blog). *Queen's Gazette*, July 13, 2020. https://www.queensu.ca/gazette/stories/discovery-thought-worms-opens-window-mind.

Chapter 9

1. Elon Musk (@elonmusk), "Varies per person, but about 80 sustained, peaking above 100 at times. Pain level increases exponentially above 80." Twitter, Nov. 26, 2018. https://twitter.com/elonmusk/status/1067175527180513280.

2. Pink, D. H. *When: The Scientific Secrets of Perfect Timing*. New York: Riverhead Books, 2019, 28–29.
3. Pink, 28–29.

Chapter 10

1. Sanbonmatsu, D. M., D. L. Strayer, N. Medeiros-Ward, & J. M. Watson. (2013) "Who Multi-Tasks and Why? Multi-Tasking Ability, Perceived Multi-Tasking Ability, Impulsivity, and Sensation Seeking," *PLOS ONE* 8(1): e54402. https://doi.org/10.1371/journal.pone.0054402.
2. Medina, J. *Brain Rules*. Seattle, WA: Pear Press, 2014.
3. Weinberg, G.M. *Quality Software Management: Systems Thinking*. New York: Dorset House, 1991.
4. Mark, G., S. Iqbal, M. Czerwinski, P. Johns, & A. Sano. (2016) "Neurotics Can't Focus: An in situ Study of Online Multitasking in the Workplace," *CHI '16: Proceedings of the 2016 CHI Conference on Human Factors in Computing Systems*, 1739–1744. https://doi.org/10.1145/2858036.2858202.
5. Pielot, M., K. Church, & R. deOliveira. (2014) "An in-situ study of mobile phone notifications," *MobileHCI '14: Proceedings of the 16th International Conference on Human-Computer Interaction with Mobile Devices & Services*, 233–242. https://doi.org/10.1145/2628363.2628364.
6. Mark, G., D. Gudith, & U. Klocke. (2008) "The Cost of Interrupted Work: More Speed and Stress," *CHI '08: Proceedings of the SIGCHI Conference on Human Factors in Computing Systems*, 107–110. https://dl.acm.org/doi/10.1145/1357054.1357072.
7. Chui, M., et al. (2012) "The social economy: Unlocking value and productivity through social technologies." McKinsey Global Institute. https://www.mckinsey.com/~/media/McKinsey/Industries/Technology%20Media%20and%20Telecommunications/High%20Tech/Our%20Insights/The%20social%20economy/MGI_The_social_economy_Full_report.ashx.
8. Coffeng, J. K., et al. (2012) "Physical Activity and Relaxation During and After Work Are Independently Associated with the Need for Recovery." *Journal of Physical Activity and Health* 12, no. 1, 109–115. https://doi.org/10.1123/jpah.2012-0452.
9. Killingsworth, M. A., & D. T. Gilbert. (2010) "A Wandering Mind Is an Unhappy Mind." *Science* 330, 932. http://www.doi.org/10.1126/science.1192439.

10. Nutrisystem. (Jan. 23, 2018) *1 in 3 Americans Can't Eat a Meal Without Being on Their Phone* [Press Release]. https://newsroom.nutrisystem.com/1-in-3-americans-cant-eat-a-meal-without-being-on-their-phone/.

Chapter 11

1. Wendsche, J., et al. (2014) "Rest Break Organization in Geriatric Care and Turnover: A Multimethod Cross-Sectional Study," *International Journal of Nursing Studies* 51, no. 9, 1246–1257. https://doi.org/10.1016/j.ijnurstu.2014.01.006.

Index

About the Author

Photo by Sarah Becker

Anna Dearmon Kornick is a time management coach, wife, and mom who helps busy professionals master time management so they can stop feeling overwhelmed and start spending time on what matters most.

As the host of *It's About Time,* a podcast about work, life, and balance, Anna shares time management tips, productivity strategies, and real-life advice to help her listeners make the most of their time. Anna's time management advice has been featured in *Forbes,* the *Washington Post, Inc.*, and *Entrepreneur*, among other publications.

Anna lives in Louisiana with her husband and two young children.